The Fifth Domain

> Wake Up Neo ...

Giuliano Pozza
John D. Halamka

The Fifth Domain - 2

INTRODUCTION

"How Real is Real?" Paul Watzlawich asked himself in a famous book. After reading the first part of this book, you will surely ask yourself, "How real is fiction?" And after reading the second part, you will probably end up wondering whether real life could be more threatening and complex than a thriller about cyber security.

A book written by two CIOs (Chief Information Officers): a novel about the breath-taking fight of Tommaso, Ned, Martin, Myriam and Diana against a destructive cyber-attack menacing the lives of thousands of patients, intertwined with real life experiences about building and managing healthcare information systems. A plot which takes place in the evocative scenarios of Rome, Florence, Malta, Canada and Odessa. As entertaining as a novel, as real as real life can be: a way to enter the world of information technology and to approach some of the big themes about security threats, IT governance, IT architectures, cloud computing and IT risks.

A note of caution: the book is for many but not for all. We strongly suggest it should be read only by anyone who happens to be a technology or an Internet user. Moreover, the book should be read and used as a call to action only by CEOs and top executives who by chance use information technologies in their companies.

PREFACE BY GIULIANO POZZA

I must thank first of all my family for supporting me and simply for being around me, sometimes quietly but most of the time as noisily as a family with two teen-agers and a small and extremely talkative young princess, never without words, could be. From the three of them and my wife I received continuous stimuli and ideas extremely important to my personal life and also, even if in a more indirect way, in writing this book. And I thank them for letting me use some of my vacation and week-end time to write, even if it was mostly time stolen from the first hours of dawn.

Special thanks to all the users and the key users (but they are all key to me!) and executives I met: I learned so much from them I would need 10 books to share it! And I cannot forget all the IT Professionals I worked with: truly it was an honor and a continuous source of inspiration for me to share with them the passion, the suffering, the failures and the successes of our work.

I want to add to my "thank-you list" John Halamka. I do not need to introduce him: he is one of the most interesting CIOs around and one of the most interesting persons I know as well, having the unique characteristics to be a technology leader, a governance expert and a physician at the same time. He did not consider my improbable first e-mail to him to be spam (the subject was, "Uncommon question") and agreed to join me in this adventure. He constantly encouraged, advised and supported me during the preparation of this book. Moreover, he provided the extremely interesting materials used for the "Life as a healthcare CIO" appendices coming from his remarkable blog (*http://geekdoctor.blogspot.com/*). In fact, the book is an intertwinement of a novel and a number of appendices ("Life as a healthcare CIO", with experiences from John's blog and FAQs & FACTS, with links to interesting news and articles). Of course I take full responsibility for the content of the novel and the FAQs & FACTS appendices: I am the only one to blame for any "bug" in the form or in the content. I am aware it could be hard to read all the book for many potential readers, but I do believe the strength of our work is in the mix of fiction and reality, with the objective to give to the reader an idea of the big IT Governance themes (and day to day nuisances) currently challenging healthcare (and not only healthcare) CIOs. Due to the background of the authors, there is probably a bias, stressing the CIO's point of view. The reader should consider this book as a sort of experiment, a proof of concept of what I proposed in my article, "Communicating IT Governance: Does it matter?" (ISACA OnlineJournal – Vol. II 2014) - *www.isaca.org/journal*). As expressed in the article, the optimal team to write a book of this kind should be composed of three or four different experts, including a CEO. Maybe somebody else could take the good ideas of this prototypal work and develop them better than we could.

I hope as well our work will not be considered a "pessimistic view" of reality: there is no intention to demonize the Internet or social media. If used wisely, they are powerful tools, as Pope Francesco shows us with his Facebook and Twitter accounts or the Dalai Lama with his website, to cite only two eminent personalities who use the Internet to spread their positive messages. There is always hope even in the dark times, but sometimes a mix of realism and madness is required to avoid being overwhelmed by absurdity and pettiness and find new ways to change reality for the best, as the characters of Don Chisciotte and Sancho Panza suggest to us in a metaphorical sense.

One last thought. The book can be read in different ways: if you want to read the novel with the full story of Tommaso Degregori, Ned, Martin, Myriam Guccini, Dr. Bennato, Angelo Conte and Diana first, it should take you no more than three or four hours' reading. But to fully appreciate the "realism" of the novel, I strongly suggest you spend some time, during the first reading of the novel or soon after it, to explore the content of the appendices: you will discover at the end that there is more in reality than you can imagine reading the novel or, as Shakespeare said centuries ago, "There are more things in heaven and earth, Horatio, Than are dreamt of in your philosophy."

Giuliano Pozza, January 6 2014, Epiphany

P.S.: I should ask forgiveness to the 24 readers who will read this novel. I'd like to say I am not an English writer, but to be completely honest, I must admit I am not a writer at all. I am a sort of CIO with some passion for IT Governance and writing. Please forgive me for writing and for writing in English, moreover ... I should admit as well I am not a security expert, and some of the digressions on security and some ideas in the book (such as the CIRANO project) must be considered as a kind of "poetic license".

P.P.S.: After I finished writing my preface, I sent it to a friend for his feedback. Since he read a first draft of the novel and he is also a professional and a writer in the IT security and governance field, I also asked him if he was not growing tired of fighting against the "dark power" of people trying to use technology for their criminal ends and the foolishness of all of us, who allow this to happen by using the technology in such a unwise way. What was the motivation compelling him to go on working and writing? I received the following weird e-mail:

Subject: Telephone numbers

Dear Giuliano,
Here are the phone numbers you were asking me for last week:
572 684 644 645   47 50 (603) 66 743
572 684 877   47 50 (285) 66 (303)

Best regards

Don't try to call the numbers; of course I did not ask him for any telephone number at all. But the guy is fond of enigmas so please, if you can solve the riddle, write me at my personal e-mail: *giuliano.pozza@gmail.com.*
I would greatly appreciate any further feedback on the book as well.

At the same e-mail you can notify any "bug" both in form and in content you will find in the book. Yes, because you are reading release 1.0 of "The Fifth Domain" and, if you had any chance to use software, you know by now three basic rules of software development:
1. Release 1.0 is ALWAYS full of bugs;
2. The "bug free" release is ALWAYS release "N+1", where "N" is your current release;
3. The software producers will ALWAYS empower you with the honor to help them to find the bugs, thus speeding up the voyage toward the mythical "bug free release".

I empower you as well with the honor to help us to improve our work writing to me a feedback e-mail. I hope these limitations will not inhibit you from enjoying your reading!

PREFACE BY JOHN D. HALAMKA

As an undergraduate at Stanford University, my Senior thesis in public policy was titled "Espionage in the Silicon Valley" (it's available on Amazon oddly enough *http://www.amazon.com/Espionage-Silicon-Valley-John-Halamka/dp/0895882256*). I spent endless hours in locked evidence rooms listening to surveillance tapes, reading transcripts of wiretaps, and studying microfilm to assemble the true stories called

1. "The Polish Persuasion" - True Soviet-bloc espionage on defense companies in Silicon Valley
2. "The Night Of MOS and Mayhem" - Stolen chips
3. "The Mask Marauder" - Stolen chip designs
4. "The Bruchhausen Connection" - transhipment of embargoed high-tech equipment to Eastern Europe.
5. "The Tokyo Transgression" - Hitachi spying on IBM

with characters like "one-eyed Jack" and actual crime scene photos of murder, mayhem, and spying gone awry.

35 years later, cybersecurity and cybercrime are part of my daily job experience. I would have never predicted that life as a CIO would include such intrigue.

Just as the technology executives in my book were often hapless victims, many CIOs do not realize what is going on around them. Some have told me that they've never been hacked and there is no evidence of malware on their networks.

A CIO who believes a breach has never occurred is simply not looking hard enough. Given the right tools and the right expertise, evidence of bad actors is easy to find. The modern internet is swamp and cyber-criminals find medical records, easily usable to commit medical identify/insurance theft, particularly alluring.

Giuliano Pozza has written a remarkable book, merging his real life experience as CIO with the real risks and vulnerabilities present on all healthcare networks. His storytelling is compelling. His message is real and should be a wakeup call to every CIO and CEO as well.

In 2013, I've added 13 new IT security staff and an additional 3 million dollars to my capital budget for security related projects. The Cold War between the hackers and the hacked is real. Now is the time to invest. Now is the time to consider an enterprise architecture and security strategy, backed by strong governance.

If there is any doubt about the reality of this book, I can tell you from first hand experience that Beth Israel Deaconess has already issued privacy breach reports to the US government about incidents identical to those in this book.

Our applications, our infrastructure and our devices are vulnerable. It's our responsibility to mitigate the risk by adding increasingly sophisticated controls. Our reputation and patient lives depend on it.

Enjoy the chapters ahead, knowing that Giuliano and I live in a world where such incidents happen every day.

John D. Halamka MD, New Year's Day 2014

CONTENTS

INTRODUCTION   3

PREFACE BY GIULIANO POZZA   4

PREFACE BY JOHN D. HALAMKA   8

CONTENTS   11

CHAPTER 1. INCEPTION: A DIFFICULT DAY. LOCATION: ROME, OFFICE OF CIO TOMMASO DEGREGORI. TIMELINE: PRESENT TIME, APRIL 16, ABOUT 7:30 P.M.   19

PART I: STORMY CLOUDS AND HAZARDOUS NETS   25

CHAPTER 2. DENIAL OF SERVICE. LOCATION: ROME, OFFICE OF CIO TOMMASO DEGREGORI. TIMELINE: PAST, EXACTLY ONE YEAR BEFORE, APRIL 16, 9:47 A.M.   26

CHAPTER 3. TEN WORDS. LOCATION: ISLAND OF MALTA. TIMELINE: PAST, APRIL 17, 20:34 P.M.   30

CHAPTER 4. THE CENTER OF THE QUADRANT. LOCATION: ROME. TIMELINE: PAST, MAY 31, ABOUT 5:30 P.M.   31

CHAPTER 5. DINNER WITH FRIENDS. LOCATION: ROME, LOCANDA DEI GIRASOLI. TIMELINE: PAST, JUNE 22, ABOUT 8:00 P.M.   35

CHAPTER 6. TOMMASO, MYRIAM AND ISAHBEL. LOCATION: ROME. TIMELINE: PAST, SATURDAY MORNING OF JULY. 41

CHAPTER 7. THE UNBEARABLE LIGHTNESS OF SOCIAL NETWORKS. LOCATION: ROME. TIMELINE: PAST, AUGUST 19, 10:20 A.M. 44

CHAPTER 8. AGAIN. LOCATION: ROME, HOME OF TOMMASO DEGREGORI. TIMELINE: PAST, SEPTEMBER 20, 5:55 A.M. 47

CHAPTER 9. TEN WORDS. LOCATION: ARCHIPELAGO OF MALTA. TIMELINE: PAST, SEPTEMBER 25, 10:32 A.M. ... 49

APPENDIX TO PART I: FAQS & FACTS 50

PART II: PREPARING FOR THE GREAT SIEGE AND THE FINAL ATTACK 53

CHAPTER 10. ARCHITECTURES. LOCATION: CANADA, TOTALHEALTH HEADQUARTERS. TIMELINE: PAST, NOVEMBER 28, 11:45 A.M. 54

CHAPTER 11. FROM THE FAR EAST. LOCATION: ROME, VIDEO CONFERENCE ROOM OF CIO TOMMASO DEGREGORI. TIMELINE: PAST, DECEMBER 24, 8:47 A.M. 57

CHAPTER 12. GIFTS. LOCATION: ROME. TIMELINE: PAST, DECEMBER 24, ABOUT 4:00 P.M. 61

CHAPTER 13. LONELINESS. LOCATION: ROME, AARON'S HOME. TIMELINE: PAST, JANUARY 5, ABOUT 7:00 A.M. ... 64

CHAPTER 14. DIANA HUNTING. LOCATION: CANADA, CIRANO (CYBER-CRIME RESPONSE OPERATION TEAM). TIMELINE: PAST, FEBRUARY 14, 6:35 P.M.   66

CHAPTER 15. PERSONNEL SELECTION. LOCATION: ROME. TIMELINE: PAST, MARCH 28, 3:15 P.M.   69

CHAPTER 16. DINNER AT "PONTE VECCHIO": AN ANNIVERSARY, TWO ODD E-MAILS AND AN ANNOUNCEMENT. LOCATION: FLORENCE. TIMELINE: PAST, APRIL 6, 8:15 P.M.   73

APPENDIX TO PART II: FAQS & FACTS   78

PART III CHASING THE ENEMY: JORNADA DEL MUERTO 84

CHAPTER 17. THE LESSON. LOCATION: CANADA, GHISA TRAINING CENTER. TIMELINE: PRESENT TIME, APRIL 16, 9:35 A.M.   85

CHAPTER 18. EMERGENCY MEETING. LOCATION: CANADA, GHISA TRAINING CENTER. TIMELINE: PRESENT TIME, APRIL 16, 10:30 A.M.   91

CHAPTER 19. SAFE HOUSE. LOCATION: CASTELLI ROMANI. TIMELINE: PRESENT TIME, APRIL 16, 20:45 A.M.   95

CHAPTER 20. UNEXPECTED DEPARTURE. LOCATION: MILITARY AIRPORT OF CIAMPINO (ROME). TIMELINE: PRESENT TIME, APRIL 17, 4:45 A.M.   97

CHAPTER 21. A CRUCIAL TRACK. LOCATION: CANADA, CIRANO HEADQUARTERS. TIMELINE: PRESENT TIME, APRIL 17, 10:00 A.M. LOCAL TIME   98

CHAPTER 22. INTERROGATORY. LOCATION: CANADA, CIRANO HEADQUARTERS. TIMELINE: PRESENT TIME, APRIL 17, 9:30 P.M. LOCAL TIME   103

CHAPTER 23. NIGHT. LOCATION: CANADA, CIRANO HEADQUARTERS. TIMELINE: PRESENT TIME, APRIL 18, 1:30 A.M. LOCAL TIME   105

CHAPTER 24. SHEILA. LOCATION: CANADA, CIRANO HEADQUARTERS. TIMELINE: PRESENT TIME, APRIL 18, 6:30 A.M. LOCAL TIME   106

CHAPTER 25. THE THIRD WAVE. LOCATION: CANADA, CIRANO HEADQUARTERS. TIMELINE: PRESENT TIME, APRIL 18, 9:30 A.M. LOCAL TIME   107

CHAPTER 26. MYRIAM. LOCATION: CANADA, CIRANO HEADQUARTERS. TIMELINE: PRESENT TIME, APRIL 18, 10:30 P.M. LOCAL TIME   109

CHAPTER 27. KERNEL SOFTWARE SYSTEM UPDATE – CRITICAL 0-DAYS PATCH N. 100813MEN-PASS. LOCATION: SURROUNDING OF ROME. TIMELINE: PRESENT TIME, APRIL 18, 11:30 P.M. LOCAL TIME   110

CHAPTER 28. EXODUS. LOCATION: CANADA, CIRANO HEADQUARTERS. TIMELINE: PRESENT TIME, APRIL 18, 12:00 P.M. (NOON) LOCAL TIME   113

CHAPTER 29. THE WHITE. LOCATION: CANADA, CIRANO HEADQUARTERS. TIMELINE: PRESENT TIME, APRIL 18, 2:30 P.M. LOCAL TIME   **114**

CHAPTER 30. SHAKIL. LOCATION: CANADA-ODESSA. TIMELINE: PRESENT TIME, APRIL 18, 3:00 P.M. LOCAL TIME   **116**

CHAPTER 31. JORNADA DEL MUERTO. LOCATION: CANADA. TIMELINE: PRESENT TIME, APRIL 18, 6:30 P.M. LOCAL TIME   **120**

APPENDIX TO PART III: FAQS & FACTS   **124**

APPENDICES FROM "LIFE AS A HEALTHARE CIO"   **131**

APPENDIX TO CHAPTER 1: HOW THE BREAKDOWN OF A CRITICAL IT SYSTEM (NETWORK) IMPACTED ON CAREGROUP HOSPITALS ACTIVITIES.   **132**

LIFE AS A HEALTHCARE CIO: The CareGroup Network Outage (March 4 2008 post)   132

APPENDIX TO CHAPTER 2: THE ZOMBIE COMPUTERS   **136**

LIFE AS A HEALTHCARE CIO: The Growing Malware Problem (November 9 2011 post)   136

APPENDIX TO CHAPTER 5: THE MARRIAGE BETWEEN BUSINESS AND IT   **138**

LIFE AS A HEALTHCARE CIO: Defining Business Requirements (December 29 2010 post)   138

APPENDIX TO CHAPTER 6: PERSONAL HEALTH RECORDS AND TWO PARTICULAR SITUATIONS — 141

HBR Blog Network: Be the CEO of Your Medical Information (March 30 2009, J. D. Halamka post) — 141

LIFE AS A HEALTHCARE CIO: Personal Health Records Use by Adolescents (May 15 2013 post) — 145

LIFE AS A HEALTHCARE CIO: A Chip in My Shoulder (December 18 2007 post) — 148

APPENDIX TO CHAPTER 7: IDENTITY IS THE KEY POINT! — 151

LIFE AS A HEALTHCARE CIO: Strong Identity Management (December 2 2009 post) — 151

APPENDIX TO CHAPTER 10: THE CLOUD NEEDS A CONCRETE STRATEGY — 156

LIFE AS A HEALTHCARE CIO: What is our cloud strategy? (December 5 2010 post) — 156

LIFE AS A HEALTHCARE CIO: Should we abandon the cloud? (May 16 2011 post) — 158

APPENDIX TO CHAPTER 11: BYOD SHOULD NOT BE "BUILD YOUR OWN DISASTER" — 162

LIFE AS A HEALTHCARE CIO: Bring Your Own Device (October 3 2011 post) — 162

LIFE AS A HEALTHCARE CIO: The BIDMC Laptop Encryption Program (July 23 2012 post) — 165

APPENDIX TO CHAPTER 15: WHAT A CIO NEEDS TO SURVIVE IS A HIGH PERFORMING TEAM — 169

LIFE AS A HEALTHCARE CIO: Characteristics of high performing teams (August 2 2011 post) — 169

APPENDIX TO CHAPTER 17: LESSONS ABOUT "IT GOVERNANCE & COMMUNICATION" BY AN OUTSTANDING CIO LEADER — 172

LIFE AS AN HEALTHCARE CIO: It is not a Job, it's a Lifestyle (November 2 2007 post) — 172

LIFE AS AN HEALTHCARE CIO: The Tyranny of the Urgent (November 11 2007 post) — 175

LIFE AS AN HEALTHCARE CIO: How to say "No" (November 19 2007 post) — 177

LIFE AS AN HEALTHCARE CIO: Time, Scope and Resources (December 4 2007 post) — 180

LIFE AS AN HEALTHCARE CIO: IT Governance (December 31 2007 post) — 182

LIFE AS AN HEALTHCARE CIO: Creating quantitative IT Governance (December 5 2012 post) — 186

LIFE AS AN HEALTHCARE CIO: Authority, Responsibility, and Risk (September 15 2011 post) — 188

LIFE AS AN HEALTHCARE CIO: How to be a bad CIO (February 26 2008 post) — 191

LIFE AS AN HEALTHCARE CIO: New metrics for CIO success (November 1 2011 post) — 195

LIFE AS AN HEALTHCARE CIO: New and Improved (May 7 2008 post) — 198

LIFE AS AN HEALTHCARE CIO: The Year of Governance (October 20 2010 post) — 201

LIFE AS AN HEALTHCARE CIO: Leading Change (December 5 2007 post) — 203

LIFE AS AN HEALTHCARE CIO: The Role I Play (January 15 2014 post) — 206

APPENDIX TO CHAPTER 25: ARE MEDICAL DEVICES REALLY SAFE? 208

LIFE AS A HEALTHCARE CIO: The Security Risks of Medical Devices (February 27 2013 post) 208

APPENDIX TO CHAPTER 28: HOSPITALS SHOULD BE ALWAYS READY FOR A DISASTER... 211

LIFE AS A HEALTHCARE CIO: Hospital Disaster Planning (July 18 2012 post) 211

AFTERWORD BY GIULIANO POZZA 214

ABOUT THE AUTHORS 217

Chapter 1. Inception: a difficult day. Location: Rome, office of CIO Tommaso Degregori. Timeline: present time, April 16, about 7:30 p.m.

It had been a difficult day, but nothing led him to expect an epilogue like that.

In fact, it had been a difficult phase in the life of Tommaso Degregori, the new IT Manager (or CIO, Chief Information Officer, as it was also fashionable to say in Italy at the time) of the Roman Clinic of TotalHealth, a large group from Canada that ran dozens of hospitals and rehabilitation centers around the world. He had been working with his team on a critical project for the past six months. The project involved the start-up of a new Laboratory system and was approved by the Committee for Information Systems in the fall, only after great efforts by Tommaso. The management of the hospital never really understood the project; after all, if a system worked, why spend time and energy to update it? Tommaso explained that the six-year-old laboratory system was outdated, unsafe, not upgradable and could not be integrated with the new information system of the Region in which the hospital was operating.

But to get the approval for the project, Tommaso was forced to sacrifice one even more important, at least for now: the re-engineering of the basic components of the architecture of the hospital information system. He knew well, but he was probably the only one in the executive team, that the IT architecture would probably be the real point of crisis for his hospital in the next years. But after his proposals to renew the architecture, there were only tiresome and unproductive discussions. Tommaso asked himself more and more often how to make it clear to the management of his hospital that without a major investment and a long-term project for the renovation of the foundation of IT, the operations of the Clinic were at risk within four or five years at the most, in addition to the security risks for the entire TotalHealth Group inherent in a patchwork architecture.

As he recalled the memory of those discussions a sense of frustration and fatigue arose in him. During the last meeting one of the executives had even suggested that the problem of the architecture was all a hype created by the information systems team to monopolize the investment budget for the next three years and that the disturbing (although still not so frequent) system downtimes were caused by the incompetence of the Information System Department or, worse, by the desire to put pressure on the leadership team with a sort of policy of no preventive maintenance. It did not help when Tommaso reminded them that the budget for Information Systems, although important, was only a small fraction of what they spent in the hospital diagnostic equipment or building renovations.

At one point the CEO of the clinic, Angelo Conte, arbitrated to stop the discussion. Conte was a good "CEO of the ordinary", but he did not like the large projects and risky businesses. If possible, he made sure to share the risks with someone else. Being an experienced manager, he realized that putting their hands to the architecture of information systems could be a risky adventure in the short term, while the risks of maintaining the current status would produce, if what Degregori said was true, a real problem in four or five years: maybe he could wait until the decision would be made by someone else at the Corporate level. To truncate the discussion, Conte said simply, "Degregori, let us see a business case of what you propose and we will evaluate it", provoking smiles of satisfaction from almost all those present at the Committee. In fact, most of them knew well that this was virtually impossible: behind the remaking of an IT architecture it was possible to produce a risk assessment or an estimate of the value it would bring to the Company, but it was almost impossible to build a solid business case from a purely economic and financial perspective. It was a way to sink, at least for now, the project.

However, perhaps to compensate for the defeat for Information System Department (since the CEO understood well that they were a strategic asset), Conte agreed to update the laboratory system: it was nevertheless a first step toward the renewal of the systems, allowing Tommaso to replace one of the most important vertical applications with a more robust one that better fit with the new architecture that (perhaps) one day they would have. The project was not complex but it was sensitive: the laboratory is the heart of every hospital, as the Group CIO Ned Wal often reminded Tommaso, and to stop the laboratory means to stop the hospital. The volume and pace of production of any large hospital are such that they cannot be managed without computerization and automation. Their hospital laboratory produced more than three million lab tests a year: manually they would be able to manage only a small fraction of them.

The slowdown of the laboratory information systems would result in delays for more than half of the hospital. In these situations Ned Wal alluded always, in a more or less explicit way, to the great project about the renovation of the laboratory system at St. John, one of the largest hospitals of the Group, of which he had been IT Manager years before. The project finished in a resounding fiasco, with the return to the old system after two weeks of agony trying to make the new one work. During those two weeks almost everything happened, including the throwing of samples of urine to Wal and his Information Systems specialists by a distressed head of the laboratory, an event that had certainly indelibly marked Wal and which in part explained his extreme prudence. Maybe things were not related, but Tommaso attributed to that professional trauma even the caution Wal always demonstrated about the re-engineering of systems architecture, which was in a way his project more than Tommaso's, because the architecture was a common problem to all the structures of the Group. Maybe Wal simply could not convince his CEO of the Group, Peter Hawk, to invest in architecture. Hawk was a totally different CEO than Conte: an ambitious entrepreneur, he loved risk and had led the prodigious expansion of the group over the past five years, through a number of important acquisitions in different countries. He was certainly not afraid to embark on a major project nor to plan for the necessary investments. Rather, sensed Tommaso, perhaps his fear was that the path and effort to create a common architecture, the foundation for flexible and secure information systems, could slow down his ambitious expansion plans for TotalHealth, at least in the short term. The architectural problems were always solved in the same way, increasing the computation capacity or using temporary patches, which then of course became permanent. And each new acquisition handled in this way weakened the group information systems a bit more.

The laboratory system go live did not work well. After a quiet beginning, in the evening during the final test phase the system started to show signs of unstable behavior. At first it was just a test case that failed, but they soon realized that the solution was not trivial. It was always like that in these cases: either you came to a solution in the first 30 minutes, or the probability of resolving the issue during the installation phase was smaller and smaller. In addition, the layers and the skills involved in an IT project are usually so many that the unexpected variables become part of each roll-out plan. Sometimes the unexpected is marginal; sometimes it is ruinous, as in that case. Having so many heterogeneous systems talking each other was certainly one of the factors that contributed to the failure of the project. At around one o'clock in the morning, after four hours of fruitless attempts to break the deadlock and after frantic phone calls between the engineers and specialists of the three suppliers involved, Tommaso had to give his team the order to activate the rollback procedure, which is the procedure that every diligent project manager prepares for, while hoping never to be forced to apply it. In short, the plan was something like: "We have failed, retreat. Let's go back to the old system." And his team, with great professionalism and without a word of regret, in the following two hours reversed the work of the previous six months and restored the pre-existing obsolete laboratory system. The next morning at 7 a.m. (actually just four hours after the end of the restoration activities) they were all working to verify that the rollback had not introduced any problems in the laboratory. Everything was functioning properly.

In these cases, Tommaso felt a mixture of frustration, thinking of so much work wasted and of the pleased comments that some executives would certainly exchange, and pride, as he was in charge of a group of professionals who were able to put the same diligence and professionalism into building as into dismantling, with the utmost care not to cause disruption to end users and to patients and without a moment of uncertainty or discouragement.

But now the day had exceeded all expectations. After a morning and an afternoon of explanations that Tommaso had to give on the failure of the project, at about 6:30 p.m. they had entered, without warning. Two men were now in his office, and they identified themselves as policemen: an agent of the Italian Postal Police and one of Interpol. He had just been ordered to collect the essentials and follow them. As if that was not enough, they communicated emotionlessly that Ned Wal had been missing for about two weeks and that his wife Myriam had been taken "to a safe place." They were not allowed to say more. But taken by whom? And safe from whom or what? He imagined Myriam already scared to death and for her a stress like that was not a good thing in general, more so in her present condition.

He was removed from his office in the center of Rome in a car escorted by two civilian police cars with sirens. They passed by via dei Fori Imperiali, where some pedestrians and cyclists turned a casual glance, probably mistaking him for a politician with his bodyguards. As they passed the ruins of Rome's republican and imperial past, he thought of his past, but focused in particular on the last year. Tommaso was not one to worry easily. He was in general rather curious, optimistic and inclined to action rather than concern. But the more he thought about the events of the last year, the more he felt worried, as well as curious. He was sure he caught only a part of what had developed behind the scenes and that much was still to be discovered. But little by little the pieces of the puzzle were returning to their places, and he really did not at all like what was appearing in his mind...

TIME LINE: PAST

PART I: STORMY CLOUDS AND HAZARDOUS NETS

Chapter 2. Denial of Service. Location: Rome, office of CIO Tommaso Degregori. Timeline: past, exactly one year before, April 16, 9:47 a.m.

Tommaso was hurrying to reach his office on time for an appointment with Fred, the IT Security consultant of TotalHealth Group. From time to time Fred worked with Tommaso and his team. While he passed in front of his assistant Sara, he heard her saying, "Tommaso, according to your calendar you should be out of office for a supplier meeting."

"Yes, but I moved the appointment to another day."

Sara replied, "Yes, but you forgot to update your calendar. You are in the wrong place again!"

Tommaso took a deep breath: caught again! Since the team was dispersed in different locations, they had started to use cloud-based collaboration tools as shared calendars, but he sometimes forgot to update them. And this was completely unacceptable for Sara: he must be where he is supposed to be according to his calendar; otherwise, he was in the wrong place! He had only two chances: update the calendar or leave the office. He heard himself saying, "Don't worry Sara. I am hurrying to my office to update my calendar so the universe will be all right again!"

He entered the office and shook his head. Sara was so stiff sometimes! But he knew Sara was right: to manage a distributed team was a complex task and doing it without some basic rules would be hell. And even the most sophisticated collaboration tools, if not used properly, were useless. So it was that Sara decided to dedicate herself to be the guardian of the shared calendars, and this was true for everybody, especially for Tommaso.

Fred was already waiting for him in his office. Here he was, a peculiar guy. Fred was an interesting blend between a geek, a Mossad secret agent and a spy story writer. He had the passion for story-telling and anecdotes of the writer. He had the appearance of a Mossad agent, the connection with the "dark side of information technology" and maybe, in Tommaso's opinion, many dark acquaintances as well.

At that very moment he was telling Tommaso about a convention held the week before in the Balkans. He was there together with the greatest military and security experts of the area. The theme was unsettling: how to get ready for the new frontier of war, the cyber war.

A few months ago Tommaso had asked Fred to hold a workshop for his team members about IT security. Fred was never a "zero impact guy." During the workshop he told many anecdotes. His activity as a security expert ranged from a convention with CEOs of big corporations to missions of "physical penetration testing", as security experts were calling them. And not a flash of self-irony could be spotted in Fred's eyes thinking of what the ordinary man associated with this kind of activities. Actually, the goal was to violate the physical and IT security of a company, usually on assignment by the company CEO.

The last time he participated in this kind of mission, he was disguised as a phone company technician and he presented himself to the reception of the headquarters of R&D of a multinational company. After three minutes, fearing a potentially serious breakdown in the telephone system, he was able to enter the open space were the main scientists were working. Chatting amiably with a couple of secretaries, Fred connected his laptop to the local network in order to "check the status of the phone connections." Nobody asked him why, to check the phone lines, it was necessary to connect to the research network, and nobody objected or asked him for his ID documents. The uniform, the fake badge and his skill in disguising himself convinced everybody. The two secretaries prepared a clean desk for him and offered him a strong and hot coffee. After 28 minutes, Fred was leaving the room, accompanied by one of the secretaries, with his laptop full of most of the data coming from the main server, where the most important research projects of the group were stored. After 37 minutes from the beginning of the operation, Fred was on the phone with the CEO of the company

The Fifth Domain - 27

to notify that "the physical penetration testing was over with full satisfaction" (again, no self-irony could be detected on Fred's side) and that he was ready for the debriefing. Half an hour later, the main executives of the company, including the CISO (Chief Information and Security Officer), were together in the CEO meeting room listening, mouths open, to Fred, who was presenting a detailed report of what happened and how he was able to bypass all the security measures.

After six hours of training and anecdotes, half of Tommaso's team reached the conclusion that the most appropriate security measure would be to shut down all the servers and computers. One of the younger technicians announced to everybody that he was evaluating the possibility of "joining the dark side of ICT." Nevertheless, Fred was helping Tommaso and his team a lot in defining a master plan on IT security to address at least the major risks. The topic was of paramount importance: even so, it was as hard to get investments approved on security as it was on architecture renewal. After exchanging a few pleasantries (Fred never talked about his private life, assuming he had one, but this was in line with his character), Tommaso called for Aaron. Aaron was his senior systems administrator, who was also in charge of important projects on the main datacenter of TotalHealth, and together they started to review the results of the security assessment Fred just completed, collecting some evidence on the security breaches of the clinic.

For a few minutes Tommaso, Fred and Aaron worked together, then Lisa and Vittorio entered the office unexpected. The two of them usually worked very well together and were the two pillars of the team, but it was really strange to see them entering Tommaso's office abruptly and interrupting a meeting: you could smell trouble from a distance. Lisa, responsible for the business critical applications, spoke first, as usual. "We are under attack."

Vittorio, the CTO (Chief Technology Officer), completed the picture. "A Denial of Service, it seems: somebody is bombarding two of our websites with dummy requests, thus saturating the server capabilities. We need to shut them down."

Tommaso was quick. "Is it about the main site or the Online Medical Report website?"

The answer surprised him. "No, it seems they are attacking the eLearning website and the Events & Congresses website."

Tommaso was relieved; they were two secondary websites with no sensitive data about patients. By now Fred and Aaron were already scanning the network. Tommaso agreed with Lisa and Vittorio to temporarily shut down the two websites and to alert all the system administrators to monitor the situation.

Abruptly Fred required Tommaso's attention. "I am observing abnormal traffic on the internal network."

"What exactly do you mean?" Tommaso asked, now more worried than before.

"Nothing special, it seems," Fred answered. "But it could be ..."

"What?" urged Tommaso.

Taking his time, Fred completed, "... it could be somebody entered our network and now is scanning us."

Now Tommaso was really worried: a Denial of Service attack on the websites was almost an ordinary event and they knew how to handle it, but an intruder in the network was something completely different. He asked, "Do you see any relations with the site attack?"

Aaron said, "Well, not directly. An attack to the front end servers cannot bypass our firewalls. Maybe the two things are completely unrelated, but the coincidence would really be weird. The attack seems to come from a powerful botnet but still I see no relation, unless ..."

Tommaso now was impatient. "Hey guys, please stop giving me half news ...finish your sentences!"

After a long pause Fred concluded, "...unless the website attack was a distraction. The real objective is different, but I am short of alternative hypothesis ..."

Chapter 3. Ten words. Location: Island of Malta. Timeline: past, April 17, 20:34 p.m.

Malta is a crucible: a little bit of Europe, a little bit of Sicily, a little bit of North Africa, a little bit of the East. You must drive on the left and you can speak either Italian or English, but the people of Malta think more like eastern people or Sicilian, depending on the context.

The mighty walls of La Valletta speak about a past of fierce battles, ended with the great siege during which 550 knights, supported by a few thousand soldiers and auxiliaries, kept up with one of the greatest army of the time, with almost 50,000 Ottomans.

From the hall of one of the oldest hotels in La Valletta, restructured in the very rooms where the Knights Hospitaller were living, the message Shakil transmitted on a ciphered connection had only ten words, "Launch platform identified: OK to phase two of operation Balrog."

Shakil was not a fundamentalist; he had merely been a clever kid in the Gaza strip. One of the leaders of the jihad noticed him and he was soon part of a new special program to train the "next generation warriors." During the training religion, ideology and cyber-attack techniques were mixed in a continuum. But that was the past. Now he really felt a free man, free to offer his talents to anybody able to pay him enough.

He closed the safe connection and went to stroll on the mighty walls. While he was walking, he could not stop thinking about the big battles of the past and the irony of history: the very island where the big army of the Sultan was humiliated by a small group of Christian knights was now the bridgehead for a new attack on the Western countries.

Chapter 4. The center of the quadrant. Location: Rome. Timeline: past, May 31, about 5:30 p.m.

Tommaso was having a meeting with Lisa, two of her analysts and Dr. Remo Bennato. The meeting started three hours ago but it had been very productive. Lisa was reviewing the requirements of a very significant project concerning a new information system to manage long-term care. This was quite new, at least in Italy, for most of the existing systems focused on acute care in hospital settings. Now, with the demographic changing, life was longer and chronic diseases were the real challenge for any health care system, besides the hospital acute care. In many cases, the patient was moving from wellness to disease without passing through a traditional hospital. TotalHealth was a pioneer of a different approach and Dr. Bennato was explaining the model, based on a continuum of care through three phases: vulnerability, fragility, and disability.

Tommaso was thinking that Dr. Bennato was a precious key user for Lisa and her team, since he was able to mix an analytical mind with a pragmatic approach and the talent to address complex problem in a holistic way and to find viable solutions. In Tommaso's mental ranking, Dr Bennato was very close to the center of the quadrant. Yes, Tommaso had the habit of organizing the users in a quadrant based on their mindset toward technology and problem-solving. The picture of Tommaso's mental quadrant would be something like the following:

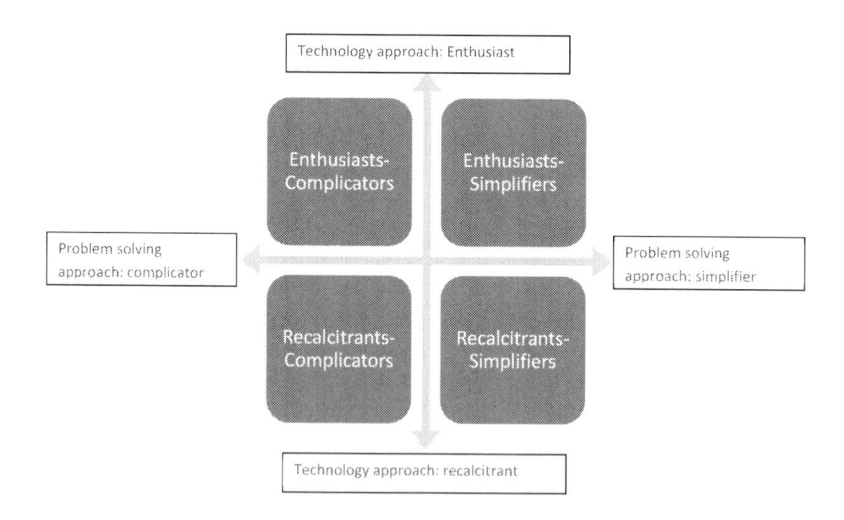

```
                    Technology approach: Enthusiast
                              ▲
                    ┌──────────────┬──────────────┐
                    │ Enthusiasts- │ Enthusiasts- │
                    │ Complicators │  Simplifiers │
Problem solving     ├──────────────┼──────────────┤   Problem solving
approach: complicator ◄─────────────────────────────► approach: simplifier
                    │ Recalcitrants│ Recalcitrants│
                    │ Complicators │  Simplifiers │
                    └──────────────┴──────────────┘
                              ▼
                    Technology approach: recalcitrant
```

In Tommaso's experience, all the kinds of users were represented. He never judged people based on their technology approach: different attitudes could be explained with different root causes and, he learned early in his career, to work with a technology enthusiast was not necessarily better. Sometimes these kind of people were prone to consider technology as the only important success factor in a project. Tommaso's experience taught him that every time a project focused on a purely technological side, it was like driving a car using only your hearing: sooner or later you are going to crash. On the other hand, a totally recalcitrant user was a problem, as well. These were the users likely to engage Tommaso and his team in dreamlike discussions about the necessity to protect the user credentials and not exchange passwords with colleagues.

In health care this was happening at every level, but physicians were often the more problematic when you tried to convince them to correctly use their personal credentials as user name and passwords. He was part of project meetings where Department Heads openly declared they were giving not only their password but even their digital signature credentials to colleagues. When Tommaso at this point usually asked, "Would you give your credit card number to your colleagues?" he wouldn't get anything more than embarrassed smiles or

The Fifth Domain - 32

statements like, "Oh, but this is a completely different situation." Tommaso spent much time explaining that access credentials and digital signatures were more important than credit card numbers: you could not be processed if you give away your credit card number, even if you would presumably experience a financial loss, while in many countries you could be under trial (and maybe even worse, you could damage your patients) for being reckless in managing your computer access credentials.

If you consider the "problem" axis, this was something Tommaso was always curious about. In fact, the "complicators", persons able to find in any situation 1000 good reasons why a solution wouldn't work and able to come out with complex and deviant solutions, were very often an important source for understanding the project risks. On the other hand, Tommaso was even more interested in the "simplifiers", the ones who theorized simple solutions to very complex problems. Undoubtedly the ability to find simple solutions to complex problems has always been one of the characteristics of genius. So any time somebody was hyper-simplifying a solution, Tommaso tried to understand if he was in front of a genius mind. Unfortunately, more often than not, it was just a matter of superficiality. Drawing from his personal experience, Tommaso was convinced that the best user was in none of the four quadrants. The ideal key user should have a balanced approach to technology and he should have a good sensitivity toward risks, but he should be able to propose concrete solutions as well, not unreasonably complicated.

Dr Bennato was a good approximation of this ideal key user. He was listening to the last questions Lisa was addressing the doctor, regarding the integration with the laboratory system. Lisa possessed the great talent to explain clearly, even to non-technical people, the technical aspects of information systems design and she knew how to listen and to understand users' requirements. To be honest, Lisa was the one on Tommaso's team with organizational and process skills, besides the technical ones. He was not able, to his dismay, to create a real "organization and processes team", but he was working with his application team to embed in any project, together with the review of technology and applications, elements of process and organization review as well.

Tommaso was considering the implications of what he was thinking when he received a call on his cell phone. Usually he did not answer calls during meetings, but when he saw Martin was calling, he excused himself and went out of the room.

"Hi Tommaso, how do you do?" Martin's friendly voice opened the call. They greeted each other and chatted for a while about their common job and how tiresome it was sometimes to collect requirements from the users: you need to be a sort of "mentalist" to read in the minds of your key users! Then Martin said, "Tommaso, I am planning to come to Rome at the end of June. What do you think if we organize a dinner on June 22? I'd like so much to meet you and Myriam again. And I admit, I need also to share with you some thoughts about some confused signals I'm sampling …"

"Yes, of course," Tommaso answered. "Can't you give me any preview?"

"Don't worry, maybe it's nothing to bother about, but I'd like to talk to you face to face."

"All right, see you on June 22, then! I'll update Myriam." Tommaso ended the call.

When Tommaso re-entered the meeting room, he was a little bit upset. Martin's allusion seemed at best strange. Anyway, the meeting was ending. Lisa was summarizing the key points, and Tommaso listened to Dr. Bennato concluding, "Thank you to everyone. I think what we are doing is really important. I always remember what one of my professors was saying: a supplement of technology always needs a supplement of soul!"

Well said; he should remember to post it in his blog. Dear Dr. Bennato, you deserve the very center of my users' quadrant!

Chapter 5. Dinner with friends. Location: Rome, Locanda dei Girasoli. Timeline: past, June 22, about 8:00 p.m.

Tommaso and Myriam arrived early at Locanda dei Girasoli. They liked that restaurant more than any other trendy place in Rome. They liked it because it was different, because the atmosphere was different and the waiters were all special and they treated you as a special person. The restaurant was close the Tuscolana street, the ancient road joining Rome with Frascati and the Castelli Romani. But this was not the reason the place was so special. The restaurant was special because it had been founded and was run by a group of parents and young adults with Down syndrome, assisted by a small number of volunteers. The restaurant was started by a small group of parents seeking to find jobs for their sons and daughters with special needs. To sit down at Locanda dei Girasoli was a unique experience, not only for the good food but for the different ambience you could experience. The time was dilated and you could take plenty of time to chat and to enjoy your dinner. Sometimes the waiters also stopped to chat and to joke among themselves or with the clients. Once Tommaso heard one of the volunteers amiably scolding two waiters for hugging each other and one of them replied, "But Luca is a friend of mine! I must stay with him as well, not only with the clients!"

They were at the reserved table waiting for Martin Hunter, the CIO of the most important clinic of TotalHealth group in Canada, close to the headquarters of TotalHealth. Martin was a good friend of Tommaso and Myriam as well, since they both worked with Martin for two years while he was in Rome as the CIO of a famous hospital in the city which started a partnership with TotalHealth. It was the first experience of TotalHealth in Italy and Martin's role had been key, not only as CIO, but more as the person responsible for the due diligences they conducted in order to evaluate the many acquisitions of clinics in Italy and in the east of Europe the group was pursuing. After two years

The Fifth Domain

Martin went back to Canada in the main clinic of the group, never forgetting Italy, Tommaso or Myriam.

Tommaso was glancing at his wife, who was in turn looking amused at two waiters chatting as if time was not relevant in that place. Myriam was really lovely that night. She was beautiful, but her beauty was always discreet, with a unique appeal to him. Her father was from Florence and her mother was from a noble family in Sicily. She had black hair and green eyes, with the strength of mind and the discretion of people from Sicily and the curiosity and sense of humor, as well as the typical accent, of the city which was the cradle of the Renaissance, where she grew up. Usually she did not dress in a showy way, but she mixed the grace of the noblewoman with the soft curves of the Mediterranean woman.

Tommaso was in the information systems team of a big hospital in town when they introduced him to his new colleague, Myriam Guccini. He was not impressed at first; she was nice but not striking. But with time he learned to appreciate her more and more. She had a unique talent: she was able to listen to you in such a total way, independently of what you were telling her. And when she was listening to you in that way ... you simply felt good. It was common after a while that colleagues and friends started looking for her advice. In many cases, she was just listening and people were able to figure out how to address the problem by themselves.

To Tommaso, after almost five years of marriage, "to be listened to" by Myriam was still something magic, primordial: he went back to the sensations of his childhood, when his mother was listening to him in amusement when he was telling her stories, boasting about his adventures with his friends. Quite often not much was real, and she knew it, but it was a game for both because Tommaso liked so much to be listened to in that way and his mother was amused and was almost nourishing herself with his enthusiasm. Maybe this was the reason way he was so bound to Myriam: she reminded him of his mother, who died when Tommaso was too young, merely 11 years old.

Tommaso was very close to his mother, with a deep link. She was a housewife who dedicated her life to her husband and family. This sometimes led her to sadness and depression. When life was too heavy, she closed herself in her room for hours, playing the violin. The execution was sad and sweet together: even now Tommaso was enchanted and moved by violin players.

Myriam did not play a violin and she was not depressed: she had a nice career and a rich social life. However, sometimes Tommaso sensed that in the depths of her eyes there was a frailty and a sadness similar to his mother's. He was so deeply in love with her weakness as well, and even more after the incident of three years ago, when he feared losing her. Myriam had a sudden sickness and soon her heart stopped beating: she was in cardiac arrest. Luckily she was working in a hospital and they saved her almost by a miracle. In that occasion they got to know TotalHealth better: while she was in hospital they discovered a congenital heart defect and the need to implant a pacemaker. TotalHealth had just arrived in the management of the hospital where they were working and where Myriam was hospitalized, and they had just started to implant a new generation of pacemakers made by Implantable Medical Devices (IMD), a company partially owned by TotalHealth. So Myriam had a new IMD pacemaker, "the best implantable technology ever: you implant it once and update it any time you need" as the commercial said.

Myriam recovered completely and went back to work in the same hospital and she stayed there also when Tommaso had the chance to become CIO in the first Italian hospital completely owned by TotalHealth. They discussed the possibility of working together again, but for now Myriam preferred not to move. Like many Italian families, with the incumbent economic downturn it was safer to work in two different companies. Besides, Myriam was just starting a new and fascinating adventure, halfway between technology, organization and processes. In fact Martin, in many ways a visionary CIO, created before he left a team called iTOP (Improvement of Technology-Organization-Processes). This was, to many experts, the new frontier of

Information systems. The idea was not new; there had been talk about it in books and articles since the eighties. But just a few were able to execute it as well as Martin: the synergic work between organization, processes and information systems was the best way to get value out of IT investments. First of all, any large project would have a Business Champion, accountable for requirement definition and for the overall benefits and objectives of the project. Then the iTOP team worked with the Champion to define requirements and follow up the project management. Any other way was false or myopic: it had been demonstrated that IT investments alone, without a clear ownership by a business executive and a review of organization and processes, together with the introduction of new technologies, could not improve company performance.

The idea came down to bridging IT and business words, and this could be done only with special teams, the "bridge builders." That was the definition Myriam used for her team. They were very hard-to-find talents: they needed a technical background to dialogue with information systems teams and enough sagacity to understand fully the business requirements. Moreover, they needed to be able to motivate people to change and to empower them. Her ability to obtain the best from other people was incredible. In the end, she used to say, who is running a process daily has all the issues in mind and possibly many of the solutions. You just need to help them with a structured approach and system thinking. The recipe was a lot of real life humble observation, empathetic listening capabilities, common sense and a little bit of methodology. Tommaso was a much different kind of CIO than Martin, the kind of CIO who was very fond of technology and with a strong technical background. Nevertheless, he experienced himself that a team like that, composed of three people, often was able to get better results than big traditional teams. Of course, IT specialists and process owners were involved in the change process, but Myriam's team was a catalyst, able to build up a new shape from entropy, a performing process from chaos.

Fortunately, though Tommaso was attracted by these kinds of reflections, the dinner was carefree and they did not talk about their jobs most of the time. Martin arrived with his wife: he was an amiable talker, who could talk about server virtualization or Medieval history with the same competence and passion. He had a technical background, but he was a CIO of the kind Martin defined as "humanistic." This was probably the secret of his ability to communicate with "the others", the non-technical guys. He was a bridge-builder as well, a translator between worlds. In recent years, he had become an opinion leader among Health care CIOs and was elected President of G.H.I.S.A. (Global Health Information System Association).

They spent the dinner talking about Rome and the historical beauties of that marvelous city with more than 2000 years of uninterrupted history. But after the dessert, when Myriam and Martin's wife went to the toilet, Martin started a strange speech. He started asking, "Tommaso, last week I was at the yearly convention of GHISA. Interesting. Many colleagues, many companies, a lot of chit-chat … but the occasion as well to see together a good number of CIOs."

Tommaso replied defensively, "You are right, I am sorry. I promised you to participate this year but … the time is quite difficult and we have so many projects ongoing …."

Martin stopped him with a gesture of his hand, "You do not need to excuse yourself. I was a young CIO before you, and I was not able to detach myself from day by day operations as I am now. I'm not here to discuss that. The point is, I collected many rumors - I would say weird rumors."

"What do you mean?" Tommaso asked.

"Maybe nothing to worry about, maybe my spider-senses are deceiving me. You know well that security attacks are almost part of our daily routine. We spend part of our time preparing or defending our systems. But …"

Here the pause was a little bit long for Tommaso's taste, so he asked, "But what?"

"Probably nothing. You know, IT is sometimes like signal analysis: not so much real information drowned in a lot of noise.

So we tend to develop a sensitivity, as in signal analysis, to identify patterns, recurring schemes emerging from noise. We do it with architecture, with design patterns, we do it when we code and we do it even in our managerial practices. And we tend to look for recurring patterns also in observing reality. To be brief, in the first months of this year it seems that many of us experienced the same kind of security attack, or at least with the same schema."

Here Tommaso could not help adding, "A denial of service attack on one or more websites and, at the same time, a scanning of internal network resources?"

Martin concluded, "Tommaso, Tommaso, I see they got you as well. If this is not a pattern, I am not Martin Hunter!"

Chapter 6. Tommaso, Myriam and ISAHBeL. Location: Rome. Timeline: past, Saturday morning of July.

"Myriam, Tommaso, it's time to wake up and to start another wonderful day!" The sweet voice of ISAHBeL awakened them, as every morning. It was strange, but in spite of the fact that her voice was somehow warm and sensual, Tommaso found her irritating, while Myriam said she was reassuring.

Tommaso opened his eyes to check the weather. From the wide windows in their bedroom the view of Rome was breathtaking. The view was dominated by Castel Sant'Angelo, the mausoleum of Emperor Adriano, which later became the fortress where the Popes took refuge in case of danger. The castle was still connected to Vatican City via the famous "passetto." Tommaso never got tired of admiring his wonderful Rome. He had been lucky: his family left him as an inheritance a flat in the very center of Rome. He could not have afforded it. As in many cities in Italy, few people could afford to live downtown, so there were more offices than families.

"Myriam, Tommaso it's time for your morning checkup," ISAHBeL said, intrusive as usual.
Myriam got up: she was so lovely with her ruffled hair and her silky nightgown. He did not know if he was more spellbound by the view of his Rome or by the perfect body of Myriam he could see through the silk. "Myriam, I'm waiting for you," ISAHBeL intruded again. He could not remember the real meaning of ISAHBeL: something like IMD Station for Administering Healthy Behavior and Living. He probably read it once on a brochure. To him ISAHBeL was an interesting but quite annoying piece of technology. The core system was composed of a footboard with an electronic scale connected via a secure UMTS connection to the IMD Operations Center. A number of optional monitoring devices could be added to check blood pressure, ECG, glycaemia and anything you could imagine to remotely monitor a person.

The Fifth Domain - 41

ISAHBeL was equipped with a state-of-the-art engine for speech recognition and speech synthesis so she could dialogue with real people in a way Tommaso found irritating and Myriam amusing. Every morning ISAHBeL collected their vital parameters and asked them a number of questions on their mental and physical state. Moreover, for patients like Myriam, with a pacemaker, ISAHBeL was linked to the implanted device through a wireless connection.

"Mainly to collect data for monitoring purposes," at least this was what the IMD technician who installed ISAHBeL told Tommaso three years before.

Tommaso could not help asking, "What do you mean exactly by 'mainly'."

The technician did not have many details to share — maybe this was part of his training — but said, "In some cases ISAHBeL could update the non-critical software components of the pacemaker."

"Well, this sound a little risky to me" Tommaso said.

"No, for sure there is no risk at all. I told you already that the critical software in the pacemaker, what we call 'kernel', can be updated only in a cardiology hospital authorized by IMD. Still, there are some minor patches regarding, for example, the information collection module of the pacemaker, which could be managed in a home setup directly by ISAHBeL."

Tommaso was not completely reassured, but ISAHBeL became to Myriam a companion, able to provide her a sense of protection. All the collected data were transmitted to the operations center and converged on Myriam's profile through a tool called TotalPersonalProfile, or TPP, a product of the collaboration between TotalHealth and IMD. TPP was a second generation Personal Health Record, meaning a collection of all your relevant health information. TPP included all the medical reports of any consultations with TotalHealth doctors, parameters about health, wellness and mental status as gathered by ISAHBeL, a personal diary where you could add pictures, messages and vocal notes integrated in your profile. In summary, TPP was a mix between a best of breed Health Personal Profile and a state-of-the-art social network. Furthermore, since TPP mixed social data with highly sensitive health data about the users, it included a sophisticated profiling access control system you could use to guarantee your contacts had controlled access to your data based on the contact profile. For example in Myriam's case, only one person could see all her data: Tommaso. The two physicians following her, the general practitioner and her cardiologist, could see all her medical data. A dozen close friends could access her personal diary. For anyone else the visibility was limited to the public aspects of her profile. Any information uploaded in TPP had a default visibility level you could overwrite freely. Myriam had been one of the pioneers of TPP and she was very fond of it because it was to her like an advanced personal diary where she could record any aspect of her life, from health status to social life and personal feelings, in a safer and broader way than a traditional social network.

Chapter 7. The unbearable lightness of social networks. Location: Rome. Timeline: past, August 19, 10:20 a.m.

Aaron was updating his profile on social networks. Yes, because Aaron, one of the brightest young engineers in the group of Tommaso Degregori, was present on almost all the major social networks. A bit for passion, a bit because of his personal history, a bit for professional reasons. The passion was born from his exuberant personality and his irrepressible desire to communicate with and relate to others. And sometimes from social networks interesting encounters and relationships were born, as the one with Sheila. His story ... well, there was a time when for him the social networks had been almost the only channel to communicate with the world. Aaron came from Israel. He was wounded and hospitalized for a long time as a child in the hospital where Tommaso was working years ago. A terrorist attack destroyed his family and left him seriously injured. He was then transferred to Italy, hospitalized, rehabilitated and then adopted by an Italian family. In those early years, social networking was his contact with the world and the passion lasted after that. The hospital was so much of his history that, after obtaining a degree in computer engineering, he submitted his candidacy as junior systems administrator in the Tommaso's group. In time he held various roles within the hospital infrastructure and systems group. The passion for social networks, however, never abandoned him. And when the marketing of some of the clinics of the group launched a massive campaign on the major social media, Aaron had been repeatedly used as an internal consultant.

Aaron and Tommaso had known each other since that time and when Tommaso moved to this new clinic, where he was appointed CIO, Aaron followed him. Somehow Tommaso became for him almost like a second father. Or maybe he should have said a third, after his natural and his adoptive father. But to them it was better not to think; they were both a source of suffering though for different reasons. Tommaso was different; he felt he was understood and not judged by him. But Tommaso was also his boss and looked with suspicion at the double life of Aaron, as a systems administrator and as a star of social marketing. Aaron suspected that this was not just a pure calculation about the time Aaron took away from his work as a systems administrator: in fact, he was tremendously efficient in his work. Tommaso had repeatedly stated that he considered it imprudent for Aaron to publish all his personal information on social networks around the world because of his role in the information systems of the clinic and the group. You could find just about anything about Aaron in the net: photos, personal history, role in information systems, links with colleagues, professional and personal interests, girls, holidays, pets ... it was enough to surf a bit between general and professional social networks. And every time Aaron told Tommaso about his adventures on the web (and their application in the real world that sometimes happened), Tommaso never failed to warn him.

At the moment Aaron was getting ready to go out with Sheila. Sheila was astonishingly beautiful. He never had problems with girls, but he had to admit that Sheila was the best he had ever had. He had known her for three months. The first contact was made through a popular social network in early May. They had been meeting for a while online, exchanging messages, information, pictures ... and then they started dating. For Aaron she was not like all the other girls: physical attraction was only part of the story. Sheila was an interesting person. She was generally very reserved and sometimes she had moments that seemed almost meditative and sad, especially when she thought she wasn't seen, but most of the time she was lively and extremely curious. Last night, for example, she had asked him how he, with all the social networks in which he participated, could possibly remember all the passwords. He had confided his trick. Each computer guy had one; it was impossible otherwise to live in a world in which counting social networks, servers, databases and other applications requires you to memorize between your private and professional life a few hundred passwords. And Aaron's trick was simple: it was enough to have a basic mnemonic phrase that you used only for the first few letters, which Aaron completed with the name of one of his girls and the year in which he had known her, periodically changing only the last part. And the sentence was taken from his favorite movie, The Matrix : "Wake up Neo, the Matrix has you." So his passwords were the initials of the phrase concatenated with the name of one of his girlfriends or ex-girlfriends (and he had plenty to choose from) and the year in which they met, the latter part separated by "# " from the rest. For example, using Elena, a girl he had met in 2011, the password would be: "WuNtMhy#Elena2011." It was a complicated rule if you did not know it, but easy to remember. There were uppercase and lowercase letters, numbers and special characters, just as recommended by each procedure on IT security.

When security consultants had made an assessment of the passwords of system administrators, his passwords were assessed by the algorithm to the maximum level of security. It's true that the consultants suggested moving from password-based authentication to a "token based" or biometric authentication, but most of his colleagues opposed the idea and he was with them: a good strategy to manage your passwords and you do not need more. Yes, if he had known, Tommaso would have told him that it was unwise to talk about his "password strategy" with a girl ... but it was Sheila. Sheila was not only a girl for him. And then he did not tell her the real names he used in his current passwords, which anyway he had to remember to change sooner or later.

Someone was ringing the bell. It was Sheila, innocent and sensual as usual! He posted the photo of Sheila as he saw her now on his online profile, on the spot, with his mobile phone!

Chapter 8. Again. Location: Rome, home of Tommaso Degregori. Timeline: past, September 20, 5:55 a.m.

"Again..." Tommaso said, lost in thought.

"Sure," Myriam said, and she started again to kiss him on the neck and behind the ears.

Tommaso smiled but did not say anything. That was not what he meant, but it was OK. It had been one of those special mornings. Myriam woke him up with soft kisses around 5 a.m. and they made love in the dawn. Those were the finest moments for him, before ISAHBeL would interfere again with their life and bring them back to the day-to-day routine. She was able to put in their moments of intimacy a mix of sweetness and passion absolutely irresistible for him. Knowing she was always so quiet and reserved in everything, who would imagine she could be that passionate? Besides, the fact that he was the only one knowing her so deeply was moving to him. Her soft and full breasts, the line of her back and hips, her neck that was so easy to kiss — all were well-known territories into which he entered every time with a mix of excitement, marvel and surprise. And now that they were trying to have a baby, those moments were sweeter and more frequent.

After quite a bit of time, Tommaso said, "Anyway, I was thinking of something else when I said 'again'."

She looked at him with mocking sulkiness and threw at him, "You rascal, you took advantage of an innocent woman! And may I at least know what were you thinking about?"

He kissed her sweetly on her lips and said, "I was thinking aloud. I was thinking that again Aaron started a story with a social network contact, Sheila."

"Ah," Myriam said, now with the jealous wife attitude, "I know her; you've shown me some of her pictures on Aaron's profile. So you are with me and you think about a sexy blond?" Now Tommaso was definitely embarrassed, but she came to his aid, "OK, let's assume you are acting in this outrageous way out of genuine interest for Aaron, right?"

"Sure, you are definitely right!" Taking the opportunity, Tommaso added, "I warned him so many times about social networks friends. And that Sheila … she did not convince me. I mean, Aaron is an interesting guy, but he is not Brad Pitt, while this Sheila …"

Myriam completed, "You do not dare to say that she is a sexy-bomb?"

"More or less," Tommaso said.

"So they started dating?"

"Yes, and quite often, I think. But at the beginning of this month she left to get a master's degree in London. Now they stay in touch on the net and they meet every month when she comes back to Rome."

She was silent for a few moments, as usual when she was preparing an answer, and she said, "Maybe you are right, but Aaron is a young man. You cannot prevent him from living his experiences and his mistakes, as well. All you can do is to be there when he needs you."

Yes, Tommaso thought, *as usual you are right, but I do feel uneasy anyway.*

Chapter 9. Ten Words. Location: Archipelago of Malta. Timeline: past, September 25, 10:32 a.m.

Shakil was lying on a deckchair in one of the most beautiful beaches in Gozo, in the archipelago of Malta. His laptop was with him and he was hooked up to a secure connection with a SIM card bought in the morning, to be thrown away at the end of the day. Close to him, his new girlfriend was sleeping with a book on her breasts. She was a stunner. This new organization was really great: easy money and the collateral benefits, like this girl, were by no means contemptible. She did not spend much time with him — she was very busy — but any time she was here she brought him important pieces of information and they would enjoy some time together.

The last message Shakil transmitted from the beach was again composed of 10 words: "Boromir hooked and deciphered. OK with phase three operation Balrog."

APPENDIX TO PART I: FAQS & FACTS

Q) What is a Denial of Service (DOS) attack?
A) A DOS (Denial of Service) attack is an attempt to make a machine or network resource unavailable to its intended users. Although the means to carry out, motives for, and targets of a DoS attack may vary, it generally consists of efforts to temporarily or indefinitely interrupt or suspend services of a host (computer) connected to the Internet.
The definition is extracted from Wikipedia:
http://en.wikipedia.org/wiki/Denial-of-service_attack

Q) How frequent are Denial of Service attacks?
A) If it holds true that a picture is worth a thousand words, an animated map is worth a billion. There is an interesting site, fruit of the collaboration between Google Ideas and Arbor Networks, showing the DOS attacks in real time and a repository of the past attacks:
http://www.digitalattackmap.com
After a few minutes on the site, you should be convinced DOS attacks are pretty frequent. Actually, they are a continuous threat to many websites worldwide.

Q) What is the meaning of "social engineering"?
A) Wikipedia is always a good starting point, "Social engineering, in the context of information security, refers to psychological manipulation of people into performing actions or divulging confidential information" (http://en.wikipedia.org/wiki/Social_engineering_(security)). **But what is becoming explosive is the use of both traditional techniques and social networks to manipulate people. The case of Emily Williams is representative. Try to google: "emily williams social engineering" or follow the links:**
http://www.thesecurityblogger.com/?p=1903
http://www.thesecurityblogger.com/?p=2161

Q) IT security? I believe it is all hype. Why should a business executive bother with it?
A) Unfortunately, real life is sometimes stranger than fiction in showing us that IT security cannot be dismissed with "it's all hype." IT security is important for business executives for at least three simple reasons:
a) Information Technology is becoming more and more pervasive and an IT service disruption has tremendous impacts on business;
b) In the absence of effective countermeasures, in the last years the cyber-attacks have become more and more dangerous, leading to increasing impacts on business continuity;
c) Top executives are accountable for what they do to protect clients' data and to prevent business disruptions.

Non-IT executives are not supposed to become IT experts, of course. But they are supposed to give the proper attention, time and resources to IT, as R. Plant writes in an HBR Blog Network article *(http://blogs.hbr.org/2013/08/it-doesnt-matter-to-ceos/).*

More about security for executives is explained in "10 Steps to Cyber Security – Executive Companion" by CESG (UK Government's National Technical Authority for Information Assurance). I'd like to mention a single sentence from the report, "Ultimate responsibility for cyber security rests at Board level". For more info google "10 Steps to Cyber Security – Executive Companion CESG" or follow the link:
https://www.gov.uk/government/uploads/system/uploads/attachment_data/file/73128/12-1120-10-steps-to-cyber-security-executive.pdf
We could add more about DATAGATE for example. If you google it, you will find a wealth of information. From one of the last articles from New York Times: "The National Security Agency has implanted software in nearly 100.000 computers around the world that allows the United States to

conduct surveillance on those machines and can also create a digital highway for launching cyberattacks".
http://www.nytimes.com/2014/01/15/us/nsa-effort-pries-open-computers-not-connected-to-internet.html?hp&_r=2&utm_source=Good+Morning+Italia&utm_campaign=b1719b5e44-Good+Morning+Italia&utm_medium=email&utm_term=0_e1b9677db7-b1719b5e44-33787889

Q) Does "Locanda dei Girasoli" really exist?
A) Yes, it does exist and it is a special place:
http://www.lalocandadeigirasoli.it/
It is located in "via dei Sulpici 117/H" in Rome (close to via Tuscolana). Locanda dei Girasoli was founded with the goal of helping people with Down syndrome to enter the labor market. It is a place you must visit if you are in Rome and you want to taste good Italian food in a warm atmosphere.

If you want to know more about how the reality can go beyond fiction, read the appendices to chapters 1 to 9 at the end of the book, collecting selected posts from John D. Halamka's blog, LIFE AS A HEALTHCARE CIO.

TIMELINE: PAST

PART II: PREPARING FOR THE GREAT SIEGE AND THE FINAL ATTACK

Chapter 10. Architectures. Location: Canada, TotalHealth Headquarters. Timeline: past, November 28, 11:45 a.m.

Ned and Fred were in a meeting with the Board of Directors of TotalHealth Group. The Board was composed of the Group CEO, Peter Hawk, and his first line of command. It was the decision-making body in charge of, among many other issues, evaluating the investment plan for common infrastructures as the IT architecture was. The meeting lasted for 2 hours, a long time for group Top Executives, and Fred had never seen Ned as enraged as now. But the pattern of the meeting was the usual one: a movie he had watched too many times in the past 5 years. Ned was proposing to rationalize common infrastructure and architectures with standard and common security measures; the CEO and the other executives were supporting a more decentralized approach. This translated to minimal common infrastructure, basically no common standard. Every location was self-managed, sharing a bunch of IT services such as e-mail and wide area network.

Ned was almost shouting when he said, "We cannot accept any more anarchy in IT governance! We are now more than 40 clinics around the globe with different standards and architectures. The situation is out of control!"

Silence in the meeting room. Hawk looked at him in an eloquent way, implying, "You are one of my trusted men, but do not exaggerate" as he said plainly, "Didn't we invest millions in the past year in common infrastructure? I think the effort, even from a purely economic perspective, has not been irrelevant."

Ned responded, this time in a more appropriate tone, "Yes, but when you speak about IT security, the chain is only as strong as its weakest link. Even if our main sites were hyper-protected — and this is not the case — if one of the secondary sites is ill-protected we have a security hole threatening everybody! Just recently I had a conference call with some of our CIOs from east Europe. You know what the CIO of Kiev told me? He said his CEO thinks ICT is too complex to be managed by his staff so he decided to outsource everything to a partner. We have no warranties on service levels or on security measures. Their rush toward the new IT trends like the cloud or the use of personal devices inside the company is without any discernment. I and Fred are almost sure the security perimeter has been violated in this very moment."

Hawk raised an eyebrow and said, "Can you prove what you are saying? Or we are just listening to your theories because you are philosophically averse to cloud computing and the use of personal devices? I think your views are getting more and more anti-historical, even if this is probably just you ..."

Ned was livid, but Fred noticed with relief that he was able to reply properly, "The problem is not my views. We know very well that Martin Hunter and Tommaso Degregori, to make an example, both use cloud service, but they do it after a careful evaluation of service level, contractual condition and security implication before they activate the services. To follow market hype without understanding the implications is something different."

Hawk replied, "Well, what are you suggesting, then? We cannot interfere with internal management of our clinics."

Ned answered, looking straight into Hawk's eyes, "Let's impose contractual and architectural standards and, in the meantime, let's limit the access to common resources by the east Europe clinic. And from now on we must perform an IT due diligence before any new acquisition."

Hawk thought for a while, then answered, "I'll think about it, Ned, but right now I do not think your idea of segregating our friends from east Europe is viable. We spent too much time and energy integrating them into the Group! Segregation would convey the wrong kind of message to the whole organization. Besides, our master plan foresees an aggressive expansion policy in Europe in the next three years and we cannot slow down now. Maybe we will reconsider your proposals in the next few years. Now see what you can do to help our colleagues in Kiev. That's it. See you at the next Board meeting."

So, to Ned's dismay, this meeting also closed without a decision. Fred was frustrated. Sometimes he thought Ned should settle for something less than the "big battle." Fred felt more like Sancho Panza: he wanted just a castle with a little bit of embedded security, while Ned was trying to change the world, just like Don Quixote. Ned turned to Fred and said: "We need to prepare: we will fly east to see what's happening."

Chapter 11. From the far east. Location: Rome, video conference room of CIO Tommaso Degregori. Timeline: past, December 24, 8:47 a.m.

Tommaso passed by the desk of his assistant Sara, who greeted him amiably and reminded him that, for the second time this week, he was in the wrong office. Moreover, he was not supposed to be in the office at all because his calendar showed clearly he was on holiday.

He was going to reply that he was there because Wal woke him up at 6:32 a.m. with an urgent call asking for a video conference at 9:00 a.m. So he was here instead of strolling around for Christmas gifts. But she wouldn't understand, so he said, "Thank you, Sara. Indeed I am on holiday, but I decided to spend my first holiday morning in the office, just to have a smooth transition from work to holidays. I'll go in the video conference room to greet some colleagues and afterwards in my office to prepare my Christmas gift list!"

Wal was in the "far east", as he said when he was leaving for east Europe two weeks ago. Tommaso joined the video conference. On the screen he could see Wal and, close to him, Fred.
In the background a glass wall showed an arctic landscape, completely covered by snow and with big flakes falling.

"Merry Christmas Eve, Ned. Hi Fred," Tommaso began. "I see you do not miss snow out there!"

"Please stop it" Ned replied in his worst mood. "We have been living among snow and wolves for the past two weeks. I cannot wait to get back to headquarters. But I needed to check with you before we leave."

"If I can help, no problem," Tommaso said genially.

Fred said, "Do you remember the intrusion I witnessed in April?"

"Sure I do, but we were never able to demonstrate it was an intrusion," Tommaso replied.

The Fifth Domain - 57

"OK Tommaso, but do you have any hypothesis on what they were looking for?"

"No, to be honest, no. But why are you asking me about it after so many months?"

"Because yesterday we had a meeting with our IT services provider for east Europe. You know here they have ... huh ... I can say quite a different policy from what you are doing. Let's say they are practicing a form of 'extreme outsourcing'. Consequently, the internal IT staff is minimal and with a serious competence shortage problem. Everything, from applications to infrastructure, is managed by a big, big outsourcing multinational company. They are partially using their own cloud, and partially a portion of the TotalHealth main data center."

Tommaso replied, "I remember very well. I met Benton, the CIO of one of the east Europe clinics, during the transition phase to the new outsourcer. I would say he was a living nightmare at best."

Fred continued, "Yes, and the nightmare is just beginning, in my opinion. Besides outsourcing, everybody here is using his own personal device on the local network, from smartphones to tablets, without any meaningful security policy. You know, it's the BYOD, Bring Your Own Device, craziness. CEOs are mad about it; they think it's a way to gratify employees while saving money on IT equipment. And to say more, you know how they push social networks. You can discover practically everything on any single employee just surfing a little bit: history, preferences, sons, pets, wives and girlfriends ... you know, all the sort of things you need for social engineering. It is not new. The difference is that in the past to discover all this information was a tiresome and time-consuming work; now it's all public. In the pilot phase one of your specialists was involved. I think he is Aaron — the one I met in Rome, right?"

Tommaso said, "Yes, and you know I was never enthusiastic about it."

Here Ned took over the conversation, "What Fred is saying is true but there is more. Our contract with the outsourcer was signed without any negotiation about contractual conditions.

The Fifth Domain - 58

They are a multinational company with a skilled team of managers and lawyers, so it was easy to get the right contract for them. Our top managers went on trips around the globe for months to see big data centers and to speak with important clients. I tried to convince the Group CEO to 'quarantine' east European clinics, without success. He said this kind of action 'conveys the wrong kind of message to the organization.' You can imagine that there are practically no real security obligations in the contract but we handed them the possibility to use cloud computing extensively."

Yes, Tommaso thought, Cloud Computing had always been one of Ned's worries. He thought, and he was right, that Cloud Computing was difficult to govern. The providers were giving you a virtual infrastructure in remote data centers, available on demand. Theoretically this could give you an interesting flexibility, but many sensitive issues such as data security were complex to define in a contract and you really needed a strong negotiation capacity, involving both technical and legal professionals, to win the match. And if the contractual table saw on one side a big multinational company and on the other a clinic in the east of Europe, there was no match at all.

Tommaso replied, "And what is so urgent about the cloud to convince you to spend Christmas Eve in that wild place?"

Ned answered after a while, "Yesterday, after two hours of investigation, the outsourced had to admit they experienced a critical security incident on one of our systems."

Tommaso asked, "Any additional information?"

"NO," Ned almost shouted. "This is the point: the contract we signed is bulletproof for them. There is no way we can force them to disclose information about their infrastructure. We do not know where the servers are: their cloud infrastructure ranges from India to Europe to the United States. The only thing we were able to discover is that the attack, after violating their systems, used a vulnerability in the VPN connecting them to our main data center, where the attackers were probably able to access our CMDB, the main database that acts as a data warehouse for all our IT assets."

The Fifth Domain - 59

Tommaso thought for a while then said, "Curious. Why should an attacker go for the CMDB and not for clinical data, for example? Are you thinking what I am thinking?"

This time Fred answered, "Yes, we thought what you are thinking: the only reason for such an attack, besides the hypothesis of a pure bullying action, is to gather information about our architecture, preparing for something else."

Now Tommaso was feeling really uneasy. He could hear Ned saying in the background, "Merry Christmas, Tommaso, and keep me updated on any strange events you notice in the next weeks!" He closed the conference.

Chapter 12. Gifts. Location: Rome. Timeline: past, December 24, about 4:00 p.m.

Tommaso and Myriam were walking along the Tiber, returning from the center of Rome to their home. As usual, Myriam insisted on buying a lot of gifts for all their friends and relatives, and they had two bags full of them. Tommaso bought mainly books, both for him and for others, especially for Aaron. Tommaso inherited from his family a library of 11,000 volumes that took up most of the space in their house, and this partially explained his passion for books. The entrance in a bookshop was always a moment of heated debate between him and Myriam. Usually she started reminding him that he was reading 5 books at the same time, and maybe it was not wise to further increase the height of the "tower of Pisa" he kept on his nightstand. He replied that there were at least 50 issues of great interest that he wanted to deepen: 5 books meant he was facing only 10% of his interests, so it seemed a reasonable percentage, perhaps even too low. Then he dived in the shelves of books and he usually emerged 2 hours later with a dozen books, saying something like "These must absolutely be part of my library." At that point she usually took the stern face of the teacher who has to educate a promising student who is too bent to be carried away by enthusiasm and began a negotiation that could last an hour, and that eventually led to reducing the number of books purchased by Tommaso to 3 or 4, but with the promise to return to visit the bookshop later.

Likewise that day a part of their time was spent in the bookshop and in the bags they transported there were at least 4 books. Myriam was satisfied with the negotiation, because Tommaso started with the intention of buying books for all their acquaintances.

As they walked toward the house, Myriam said, "I saw that you bought more books about IT Governance and Security than usual."

Tommaso smiled. "You are a great observer, Watson. Yes, you are right."

"And why, my dear Sherlock, if I may ask?"

Tommaso became thoughtful and told her what Ned told him in the morning during the videoconference. He told her also what Martin's conversation when they met at "Locanda dei Girasoli".

"So our modern Sherlock is on the trail of an international intrigue? A case of cyber-attack?"

"I do not know," Tommaso said. "I'm confused. But there are definitely issues on which I would like to know more. I am also subscribing to the next course of IT Governance & Communication organized by GHISA that will be held by Martin in April. Don't you sometimes have the feeling that there are things that are ... running out of hand in IT? Well, I know you are not in IT, sorry..."

"True , "said Myriam. "I do not feel like an IT girl. I do a job of translating between the computer world and all the others. And honestly, I do not know if things in IT are running out of hand. For sure I see a huge communication problem, and I am pleased that Martin put together in his course governance and communication. You IT guys talk in your own language and sometimes you give the impression that you live in your own world. This makes it tremendously difficult for normal people to understand the reasons behind the alternatives you propose. It happened to me recently on a project: users sponsoring one solution, while all the IT team disliked it and proposed another one. When we tried to investigate the reasons, they came out with at least 2 dozen words and incomprehensible acronyms: from 'architectural constraints' to 'ITIL best practices', passing through 'MOLAP' and 'RDBMS', 'BC requirements' and more. Their speech was something like: 'The two solutions are both feasible, but there are a number of architectural constraints that must be considered. Moreover, the choice between MOLAP architecture and a RDBMS is not indifferent and we believe that for the current project, the second provides a better assurance of compliance with requirements of BC and let us have a maintenance cycle post go-live closer to ITIL best practices.' I assure you that even I, with my technical background, was in deep pain trying to follow them. Imagine the medical staff."

Tommaso could not help but smile thinking about how many times he took refuge behind acronyms and technical terms. He then asked, "And then what did you do?"

Myriam replied, "Simple. I took their guy responsible for the infrastructure and their applications guy, I locked them in a room and I listened to them for about an hour and a half. At the end, I was able to extract a concept communicable to us mere mortals. The solution provider we are working with on the project has good experience with some technologies, those proposed in the solution sponsored by the IT team, and not on others. Since IT guys already tried in the past to force the same provider on unfamiliar technologies with disastrous effects, they did not want to repeat the experience that would have negative effects both in the design phase and post start-up. In particular, they were concerned about the post go live, both for impact on their team and for the real ability of the supplier to ensure continuity of service as required. So at this point the choice is between the solution proposed by the IT guys with the current solution provider or the choice of another provider if we decide to go for the alternative solution. Don't you think it is more understandable to ordinary mortals?"

"Yeah," Tommaso said, "it was just a matter of translation."

Chapter 13. Loneliness. Location: Rome, Aaron's home. Timeline: past, January 5, about 7:00 a.m.

It was their first day together for the holidays and Sheila was still sleeping. She was turned on her side but he could see, under the thin sheets, the statuesque beauty of her body. Aaron was enchanted by her every time she came back. He softly stroked her blond hair, her face, a perfect blend of innocence and sensuality, her breast and her hip, and at the end he nestled close to her, embracing her body. Aaron liked so much the tender moments after they made love or before they got up, but Sheila was more prone to sleep afterward and, after falling asleep, to wake up. This was troubling him a little bit but … when they made love it was … fantastic!

Aaron was not a boy without experience. Since he moved on after the period of total closure to the world, when he was a teenager, he dived into life with cupidity. He had taken every fruit, he lived every relation as a way to demonstrate he was worthy to somebody. And once he was reassured about it, he would pass to the next girl. Maybe to be abandoned and to abandon were two faces of the same coin. It was a rule of life, no point in despairing about it. This was one of the reasons for his troubled relationship with his adoptive family, but what could they possibly understand? To them he was still the fragile child, shattered in body and mind from a tragedy bigger than he could bear, who needed to be reassured and cared for.

Now he was a man, and nothing could make him feel reassured and cared for than a beautiful girl in his bed. But with Sheila, he had to admit, it was different. Eight months passed after their first encounter: the longest relation ever for Aaron and he was feeling bonded to her every day more. Unfortunately, he could not avoid sensing that for her it was different. To be clear, the sex with her was extraordinary. She had, he would say, an incredible "technical" ability. But he felt she was not truly involved. They talked a lot but, to be honest, she was not telling too much about herself, about her life or her past. The only personal information he collected, after he noticed a small scar and a bulge in her abdomen, was the fact that she was diabetic. They implanted a tiny insulin pump one year before in her belly. As a coincidence, the pump was made by Implantable Medical Devices, one of the biggest companies in the world producing implantable devices and partially owned by TotalHealth. After the implant, she said, she stopped feeling like a slave to insulin injections.

Now that she was taking her master's degree in London, they could meet only every 1 or 2 months or during vacations like now. During those periods they made love, spent time together, enjoyed themselves ... but Aaron could still sense a barrier. He perceived in Sheila a fragility similar to his own, so he respected her silence and her time. He tried not to notice the strange phone calls she received from time to time. She was the only person he knew with her smartphone always protected by a password. Tommaso and Wal, with their fixation on security, would be proud of her. They tried to impose encryption and passwords on smartphones for all their team members. But now the flow of his thoughts was interrupted by a kiss on his neck. Sheila was awakening and she was looking for him ... and he did not want to miss these moments of intimacy before the next abandonment.

Chapter 14. Diana hunting. Location: Canada, CIRANO (Cyber-crime Response Operation Team). Timeline: past, February 14, 6:35 p.m.

After a time during which different monitoring entities emerged spontaneously, some limited to specific business areas such as banking, at last the CIRANO project of the government of Canada was born. The CIRANO team (Cyber-attack Incident Response and Action Network Organization) was now starting to work properly. It was created as an evolution of traditional CERT or CSIRT organizations, created in many countries to monitor IT security threats. CIRANO was a network organization showing a real life example of collaboration between IT experts and agents from different governmental agencies and thanks to it Canada was a leading country in cyber security. Obviously, it was initially a kind of nightmare. In the beginning special agent Diana Simpson thought that the weird group composed of agents, IT guys, and IT agents was one of the best allies of cyber-criminals.

Not only they were ineffective and quarrelsome, but they conveyed the false impression of being able to protect the country, when they could not protect anything or anybody. Everything changed when Thomas Rowling became the CIRANO Director. Thomas worked so much on team building. He made it a point to teach them how to know and value each other before they started collaborating. He knew well that many of his team members were among the most skilled cyber-experts (or cyber-criminals; the difference was subtle sometimes) in the country and maybe in the world. Others were agents with breathtaking resumes. Their problem was simple: they spoke different languages and they were basically individualists, like many star players. After 6 months spent on team building, team management workshops and weekends in lonely mountain retreats, the result was a high performing team. Only two of them did not embrace the new spirit and Tom was inflexible with them: they were removed. Thomas used to say that team play was everything, and for it he was ready to sacrifice even a prodigy.

Diana had been in the CIRANO for two years. Up to that point hers was just a brilliant career in police, nothing more and nothing less. But she had not had the possibility to work on what was really moving her. And when Diana was moved by something, she never gave up. Sometimes her physical aspect induced other people to underestimate her: a pretty young woman with a fragile appearance was not the common stereotype of a special agent or of a cyber-crime expert, and she was both. She was a tiny girl with very black, short hair, as agile as a cat and as determined as a tiger could be. She also had a quite uncommon intuition, a photographic memory and the ability to penetrate almost any kind of information system.

Now she was on the phone with Luc, her boyfriend, to excuse herself since she was still in the office and it was St. Valentine day. It was not the first time in the past few weeks, but fortunately Luc was very understanding. There was no particular reason to stop in the office now, but her instinct was saying something was moving in the underground CIRANO was monitoring. The agents infiltrated the most important illegal websites, used by the criminals to sell and buy credit card numbers, access credentials to servers and security systems, sensitive data of any kind, viruses and malware, and in the last months they were showing interesting signs of increased activity. Diana was convinced that most of the traffic was just entropy: business as usual or "noise" created to cover something. But to cover what? Or it was just the case that cyber-crime was growing? Both hypothesis were upsetting to her. Some clues seemed more interesting than others, but she could not find a solution to the riddle. A few days earlier a colleague of the codes & encryptions section deciphered a message reminding her of "The Lord of the Rings." The word "Balrog" emerged more than once. She faintly remembered the movie Luc insisted she watch. Before she felt asleep, as usual during a movie, a monster with that name was fighting on the video. Quite often the criminals were using novels or movies to communicate, but the code was opaque to her. After two more hours she decided to go back to Luc. Without a clue she would never see the picture in the puzzle, and maybe this was the goal of the guys behind all the traffic she was analyzing. Tomorrow morning she should remember to post a request for contributions with an alert on the CIRANO website for all the partners.

Chapter 15. Personnel selection. Location: Rome. Timeline: past, March 28, 3:15 p.m.

Tommaso and Vittorio were entering the third interview that day. After the last stormy staff meeting, where Tommaso tried with some difficulty to reconcile different points of view of the sub-area managers in his organization, they decided to proceed with the selection. During the staff meeting Tommaso told them the content of the last call he had with Wal shortly before Christmas. It took him a while to decide to share it with his managers, but he eventually decided it was better to put them apart. At that point some of his managers had strong opinions about the opportunity to manage security in a more structured way. But some of them were on the opposite side of the river: they thought security was an issue above their level, an entry on the Group CIO's Agenda. If they had the chance to insert a new team member, they should aim at strengthening the critical areas. The debate was quite hot. Tommaso took some time to observe how it was proceeding: his was a good team, but they had not worked together for a long time and it was crucial to him that they could learn how to openly confront each other in a dialectic but positive way, without anybody feeling bad because his or her opinion was rejected by the team. On this point they worked a lot during the past year and they took a specific training, as well. The best trainers used many different techniques to teach a team how to dialogue: it seemed so easy, but to manage people with so many different kinds of trainings and attitudes was almost an extreme sport. In fact, after all these years working with different IT teams, Tommaso was more than ever convinced the IT professional simply did not exist. There were many kinds of professionals with some common background, but between a business analyst and a system administrator or between a service desk operator and a business intelligence expert, you could hardly find anything in common, with all due respect for all the certification bodies in the world who were trying to design career profiles for the different IT professionals.

This was evident also during the staff meetings, where Tommaso was often forced to bring together quite different views, as the ones from Vittorio, the head of infrastructure, and those of Lisa, who was in charge of applications. It was like herding a flock of cats. Anyway, they worked very hard on communication and on team building and something started to surface. But the voyage was not short; 2 or 3 years were typically necessary for building a high performance team, so their journey was just at the beginning.

That's why during the selection of new team members Tommaso was very focused on soft skills and personal profiles. For him an open mind, ready to change, was invaluable; otherwise it was impossible to dialogue. Moreover, the aptitude to think and to think before acting, the team working attitude, the holistic vision and the focus on value and execution were all landmarks to him. He once tried to represent all this with something like a flower:

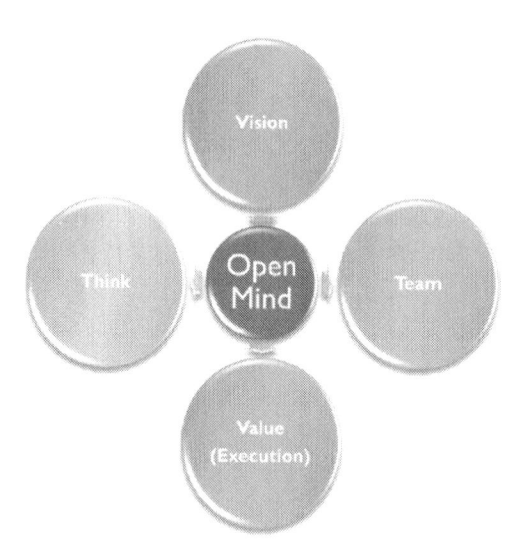

For example Vittorio, the head of infrastructure, who was assisting him during this selection, was a middle level technical expert, nothing exceptional. During the selection for the infrastructure manager Tommaso interviewed at least four who were more technically sound than Vittorio, with more vision and better technical capabilities. But technical capabilities were not so difficult to find among the consultants. What was really a scarce resource was the main characteristic of Vittorio: his open mind, always ready to question himself, his tendency to think before acting, carefully evaluating consequences of what he was going to do, and his team player attitude.

Now, after three interviews with three security experts, Tommaso concluded that no one was showing even the slightest sign of the qualities he appreciated in Vittorio. He had to admit security was a field where a new genetic mutation was in sight. He worked quite often with Fred, but he was well aware Fred was an exception. The 3 security guys they interviewed were an example of the "dark side of the strength" which was always present in IT: some of them were showing clear signs of delirium of omnipotence, with the second one close to paranoia. What they had in common was a strong focus on security, a totally incomprehensible jargon and remarkably nonexistent team working aptitudes.

One of them conditioned his willingness to work with Tommaso to a minimum level of budget for security projects, and he invested more time in negotiating this point than his own salary. Two of them were not able to express a single valid argument to communicate to top executives to convince them to invest in security, besides dark threats and dark omens of impending disaster.

Only one of the three was able to frame the European and Italian context regarding privacy and data protection and corporate responsibility. This guy was the one Tommaso liked most, but unfortunately, according to Vittorio his technical skills were not deep enough. After one morning and half an afternoon wasted, Tommaso and Vittorio decided they needed to find new interview applicants.

At the end of the day Tommaso took a few minutes to have a look at Myriam's profile on the Total Personal Profile. He did this from time to time, just to be sure everything was all right and that Myriam was not under too much stress for her fragile heart. But in the past months he started doing it with a special interest, above all for the section where she was recording her menstrual cycle.

He was now noticing an interesting anomaly, but he saw a digital post-it from Myriam, who wrote, "Tommaso, I bet your curious eye will not miss this little delay in my cycle. But you know I have never been perfectly regular, so do not fool yourself." He answered with a post-it saying, "Let's put it in the right perspective: if this is a true delay, I'm the happiest man in the world because it means we will have a baby. On the other way, if it is a false alarm ... I am the happiest man in the world because it means I have in front of me many interesting nights where we will try to have a baby ... what more can I ask from my life?"

Chapter 16. Dinner at "Ponte Vecchio": an anniversary, two odd e-mails and an announcement. Location: Florence. Timeline: past, April 6, 8:15 p.m.

It was an established tradition: for their wedding anniversary Tommaso and Myriam used to go back to Florence, where she lived as a child and a teenager, where they married and where he liked to take refuge when he could not take any more of his beautiful, indolent and chaotic Rome. Florence was on a human scale: you could cross the old town in a few minutes; even its art was less exuberant, more concentrated. In Rome you could find everything, layered in different ways, here everything revolved around the amazing years of Humanism and Renaissance.

As usual, they were staying at La Scaletta, a bed and breakfast close to Ponte Vecchio. They were having dinner on the terrace and the view, even if not new to them, was breathtaking: on the landscape towered the dome of Brunelleschi, Giotto's bell tower and Palazzo Vecchio.

Myriam's eyes were charming by candlelight, but this time Tommaso was not enchanted as usual. Actually his mind was lost in distant thoughts. It's usually part of the capacities of people very good at listening to sense immediately when they are not listened to themselves, so Myriam said casually, "Tomorrow I'll leave for Melbourne." And when Tommaso replied only, "OK, well", looking at the horizon, she stopped eating the wonderful spumoni cake with almonds and said, "Tommaso, let's stop for a second: you have been talking to me in monosyllables throughout dinner and you are barely listening to me." He looked bewildered: it never happened to him to be so absent-minded during a lovely dinner with Myriam. She looked at him and burst out laughing. "You really should see your face now! You look like a child caught with his hands in the cookie jar! So now I am really interested: tell me who has the power to divert your attention from me in such a way?"

He sighed and said, "Sorry Myriam, but it's Ned."

More soft laughter. "So you are not thinking about a new sexy colleague? Ned has this power? I am indignant!"

He kissed her hand and took out from his pocket two e-mails he printed that morning. "It's about a strange situation. You know that, after the Christmas eve videoconference, Ned had been more and more difficult to find. I last saw him 10 days ago. He was passing by Rome and he was going back to visit our east Europe clinics. He was visibly worried, distraught; he was saying he was after something, but he did not tell me what. In the past 3 days I tried many times to get in touch with him but without success. You know this is quite uncommon for a guy like Ned. And today I received two peculiar e-mails, one on my job e-mail and one on my personal e-mail. Read them yourself."

FIRST MAIL (from Ned's company e-mail to Tommaso's company e-mail):
April 6 -time: 11:34 a.m.
from: Ned Wal
to: Tommaso Degregori

Subject: Telephone number

Dear Tom,
here is the phone number you were asking me last week:
(+39) 24 58 80
Best regards
Ned

PS: Next time I'm back at Headquarters, I'll remove the encryption from my laptop. I think it is slowing down the processor too much ...

SECOND MAIL (from Ned's personal e-mail to Tommaso's personal e-mail):
April 6 - time: 11:34 a.m.

The Fifth Domain - 74

from: Ned Wal
to: Tommaso Degregori

Subject: Social Networks

Dear Tom,
I have been thinking a lot about social networks in the past week. You know, I told you once that you fly too high on some topics, and this is probably one of those. But after considering the evolution of society, I think we should experiment more with the power of social networks. You could be a pioneer with your group. Don't be amazed by my new attitude on the subject: old people sometimes are fools, sometimes are wise ... Besides, you know, I discovered that social networks are extremely useful if you want to know somebody better. There is so much information about all of us out there I could hardly imagine before. My greetings to your wonderful wife Myriam.

See you soon
Ned

Myriam was lost in thought for a while, then she agreed, "Two odd e-mails indeed. But we both know Ned is very, very peculiar. Besides being an eccentric, avid reader like you but with a strong inclination toward worlds without technology, you told me that sometimes he looked almost scared by technology. Do you remember when we introduced him to Don Carlo? And do you remember how well they fit together, convening on the absolute need to fight against 'the dark side of technology'? You know they are still working together? One day we should visit Don Carlo; maybe he will give us a hint on what is really going on in Ned's head. Or maybe Ned was just trying to give you a telephone number and to send you a thought about the evolution of man and knowledge."

Tommaso shook his head. "I don't buy your explanation. First of all, I did not ask him for any telephone number. Besides, I tried to call the number but it does not exist. Third, in his first e-mail he said he is going to deactivate the encryption on his laptop. Can you imagine? Ned made it a point, and he carried it on with a global battle, to impose encryption to all the Top Executives' laptops. They almost fired him for this battle! And the second mail was even stranger than the first: he praises the social networks, 'We should experiment more with the power of social networks'! Do you remember what happened during the last top executives meeting in Canada? I was not present but it's already a legend in the company. As usual, the top executives were using their tablets and smartphones even during the meeting to stay connected. This approach leads quite often to lengthy meetings because the majority of the participants are not really present, they are somewhere else. During the last meeting Ned made a speech on the risks of social networks, threatening to prohibit their use inside the company, and he stressed it was useless to hold 3 hours meetings where half of the participants were surfing the 'net all the time. The executives were so embarrassed nobody dared to look at his tablet or smartphone any more. Later on, he convinced the group CEO to publish a policy called 'weapons on the table': at the beginning of each meeting everyone must put smartphones and tables in the center of the table and they can use them only for real emergencies. This happened no more than a month ago! And I don't remember if I told you, he is part of an NGO organizing courses for teenagers on conscious use of technology. They called it the SUOT Team, meaning team for "Savvy Use Of Technology." They have even a website. And now you are telling me he is embracing social networks? And why should he write me two e-mails on my job and personal e-mail at the same time? I told Martin about it on the phone and he agrees with me that he finds Ned's e-mail and his behavior in the last period quite strange. But he has no explanation either."

Myriam took his hand and said softly, "Do you remember the movie we saw recently on illusionism? There are things you cannot understand if you look at them too closely. Maybe you should distance yourself and you will see better. But now your 'wonderful wife', as Ned was reminding you, is claiming you!"

They got up and strolled through Ponte Vecchio. They followed Arno at first, passing by Galleria degli Uffizi, and reached Palazzo Vecchio. Now Tommaso was really at peace. He was breathing in the beautiful city and he was breathing in Myriam, who was holding his hand while at every corner she was telling him anecdotes from Florence's history.

It was night when they walked back to their hotel. While they were crossing Ponte Vecchio, Myriam stopped. Tommaso embraced her and she said, "Easy now, you must be careful when you hug me." Tommaso looked at her in surprise, seized with doubt or an intuition. When she saw a faint smile lighting his face, Myriam gave him the best news of that difficult year. "Yes, my dear and busy CIO, you were right when you suspected me for the last delay: I am guilty, and I think now you should handle me with great respect and caution. We will have a baby!"

Tommaso could not speak any more, so he embraced her tenderly and they stayed there like two fools, on the most beautiful bridge in the world, waiting for their joy to melt down in a communion if possible even deeper that what they experienced before.

APPENDIX TO PART II: FAQS & FACTS

Q) Why is IT architecture important?
A) *The best answer I found to the question is the one from OpenGroup: "An IT architecture provides the necessary technical foundation for an effective IT strategy, which is the core of any successful modern business strategy. [...] Specifically, an IT architecture defines the components or building blocks that make up the overall information system. [...] An effective IT architecture is critical to business survival and success, and is the indispensable means to achieving competitive advantage through IT. Today's CEOs know that the effective management and exploitation of information through IT is the key to business success. An IT architecture addresses this need, by providing a strategic context for the evolution of the IT system in response to the constantly changing needs of the business environment. [...] In short, an effective IT architecture can make the difference between business success and failure. By investing in IT architecture, you are investing in business success, independence from suppliers and control over your own destiny"* (**http://www.opengroup.org/public/arch/p1/oview/**).
Many executives like to have the "big picture": IT architecture is the "big picture" about the present and the future of enterprise IT. If you miss the big picture, you will fail even if you manage the details exceptionally well ... Besides, a bad architecture, as shown in the novel, can lead to complex IT management and security vulnerabilities. To cite another good starting point to explore the link between IT architecture and business strategy and execution, a good IT architecture is a "foundation for execution" (Ross, Weill, Robertson, "Enterprise Architecture as Strategy" – Harvard Business School Press).

Q) IT is expensive, too complex to manage and it is not our core business. Why don't we outsource everything?

The Fifth Domain - 78

A) The first answer here is: you cannot outsource what you do not know and hope you will get any benefit from it. Moreover, managing an outsourced IT is in many ways more complex than managing an internal IT function. So the reason to outsource should not be searched for in "complexity" or purely in "cost saving" objectives. Even if IT is not a core service for a company, it is probably an enabler of many core services. The outsourcing decision should be linked to enterprise strategy, as is explained, for example, in Danis Chamberland's article (search "Chamberland outsourcing" on *http://iveybusinessjournal.com/* or follow the link: *http://iveybusinessjournal.com/topics/strategy/is-it-core-or-strategic-outsourcing-as-a-strategic-management-tool#.UrxiiPTuJ0w.)*

It is clear that the decision of what should or should not be outsourced cannot be made by a single actor: the CIO and the CEO (or the board) have both only partial information necessary for a right decision.

One more note: the skills and the competencies needed to manage an outsourced IT are completely different from the ones needed to manage an internal IT. A good project manager with no experience in contract negotiation and management could be valuable in an internal IT department, less strategic if most of the IT functions are outsourced. More about outsourcing risks can be found at:
http://www.isaca.org/Journal/Past-Issues/2005/Volume-5/Pages/Outsourcing-A-Risk-Management-Perspective1.aspx
or searching for "outsourcing" on ISACA website *(http://www.isaca.org)*

Q) Now that we have the Cloud, why should we invest in our private infrastructure?
A) First of all, let's start with the definition of Cloud Computing, a task not easy indeed.
Gartner defines public cloud computing as *"a style of computing where scalable and elastic IT-enabled capabilities*

are provided as a service to external customers using Internet technologies—i.e., public cloud computing uses cloud computing technologies to support customers that are external to the provider's organization. Using public cloud services generates the types of economies of scale and sharing of resources that can reduce costs and increase choices of technologies. From a government organization's perspective, using public cloud services implies that any organization (in any industry sector and jurisdiction) can use the same services (e.g., infrastructure, platform or software), without guarantees about where data would be located and stored."

As for outsourcing, the Cloud approach should start with a strategy developed by the CIO and CEO / Board of Directors. A few companies have a cloud computing strategy. An interesting example is the UK Government Cloud Strategy:
https://www.gov.uk/government/publications/government-cloud-strategy.

To learn more about cloud computing, a good starting point is Wikipedia:
http://en.wikipedia.org/wiki/Cloud_computing

In the same article you can find definitions, benefits and issues with cloud computing. The final part of Gartner's definition states that clients of cloud services should expect no "guarantees about where data would be located and stored." Again, the point is not about technology but business strategies: what kind of data would a CEO/Board like to manage internally? What kind of data/services could be managed in the cloud? What are the pros and cons of the different choices? What are the risks of buying cloud services by providers and what guarantees should be embedded in the contracts? How should one define, for example, way-out policies to avoid vendor lock-in?

An interesting initiative is G-Cloud by the UK Government:
http://en.wikipedia.org/wiki/UK_Government_G-Cloud

The program includes both framework agreements with suppliers, mitigating the risks associated with procurement of cloud services, and an online store of certified applications.

A final thought: the extreme solutions are often the wrong ones. The point is not to decide if a company should use cloud computing or not. Cloud is a reality which can give important benefits to many companies. But there are risks to be aware of as well. Many experts are sponsoring a "hybrid cloud" as an interesting solution. Gartner defines a hybrid cloud service as a cloud computing service that is composed of some combination of private, public and community cloud services, from different service providers. This sounds nice, since it gives a company the flexibility to manage its data and services in different ways: some data/services could be totally internal, some moved to external cloud providers with different service and security levels. Again, the dialogue between CIO and CEO is necessary to define a strategy before analyzing single solutions or vendors.

Q) How can I measure the benefits of my IT investments?
A) This is a complex question and it requires an answer more articulated than is possible in this context. I'll start by saying that the most mature frameworks do not speak of "benefits" but of "value", which is a broader definition. The implied point here is that to measure the financial benefits of an IT investment is possible, but it is often restrictive, especially if the measurement applies to big infrastructure and architecture investments. There is an interesting framework from ISACA, ValIT, which tries to approach value measurement in a structured way, also linking, whenever possible, infrastructure investments to business objectives. You can find more information searching ValIT on ISACA website (*http://www.isaca.org*) or following the link:
http://www.isaca.org/Knowledge-Center/Val-IT-IT-Value-Delivery-/Pages/Val-IT1.aspx
It is a starting point ... and value measurements are strictly connected to IT Governance.

Q) What is IT Governance and why is so important?
A) IT Governance is defined as follows by IT Governance Institute: "IT governance [...] is an integral part of enterprise governance and consists of the leadership and organizational structures and processes that ensure that the organization's IT sustains and extends the organization's strategies and objectives." More resources can be found at: *http://www.itgi.org/*
But I think other authors (Weill, Ross, "IT Governance: How Top Performers Manage IT Decision Rights for Superior Results" – Harvard Business School Press) have a strong point in underlining the importance of IT Governance when they say, "Effective IT Governance is the single most important predictor of the values an organization generates from IT." Another book dealing in a less conventional way with IT Governance is, "Adventures of an IT Leader", by Austin-Nolan (Harvard Business Press).

In one single sentence: no IT Governance, no value from IT!

Q) Is it possible to define what is an "IT Professional"?
A) It's hard, very hard indeed. First of all, IT Professional is too vague as a category, so we will probably need to split it down into pieces. But the issue is a hot one. Historically, IT was a field open to everyone, and this tremendously helped the innovation in recent years. Now many companies and institutions are trying to "draw the borders" of specific IT professionals. Besides the vendor certifications, there are a number of organizations trying to define certification paths. HIMSS *(www.himss.org)* is one of them for healthcare IT, for example. A more general approach is the one followed for example by the European Union with eCF framework: *http://www.ecompetences.eu/*. The framework defines 23 profiles of IT Professionals. It is still not enough, still under development ... but it is a starting point nonetheless.

PS: there is a movement trying to "certify" the IT users as well. See, for example, ECDL foundation (http://www.ecdl.com/) for more detail.

If you want to know more about how the reality can go beyond fiction, read the appendices to chapters 10 to 16 at the end of the book, collecting selected posts from John D. Halamka's blog, LIFE AS A HEALTHCARE CIO.

TIMELINE: PRESENT

PART III CHASING THE ENEMY: JORNADA DEL MUERTO

Chapter 17. The lesson. Location: Canada, GHISA training center. Timeline: present time, April 16, 9:35 a.m.

Martin Hunter, as usual, had turned his cell phone off at the beginning of the lesson. He had just started the "IT Governance & Communication" course at GHISA headquarters. The course included on-site students and online ones via videoconference, as well. Among them was Tommaso, who tried never to miss any lesson from Martin. Besides being a friend and his mentor, Martin was probably the best communicator he had met in the technology area and maybe ever. The lesson was part of a training curricula for Chief Information Officers and for future CIOs, leading to an international certification. It was one of the recent GHISA initiatives, strongly supported by Martin, to strengthen the skills and competencies about governance and communication of high potentials in health care IT organizations.

Before they started, Martin greeted all those present and informed them that all the materials would be posted on GHISA website. At the beginning of the lesson, the silence was almost religious. As he did often, he started with a paradox. "Dear colleagues, you know well this course was designed for CIOs and candidate CIOs. Now I apologize, but I must give you really bad news: the role of Chief Information Officer is gone. To be clearer, the CIO role is old, inadequate. And you know what? While I am saying it, I am fully aware of the difficulties we have in training competent and effective CIOs, because a good CIO is a mix of vision, technical and managerial competencies, leadership and communication skills. But what I am trying to say is that a good CIO is not enough. I'll try to prove my statement in four points.

"First of all, we have a complexity issue: the world in recent years has become more and more high-speed and interconnected, and IT had a central role in that. Some authors are saying that, up to a few years ago, an average of 20% of the processes in a company were digitized. Now in most companies 50% or more of the processes are digitized. This means greater efficiency but more frailty and instability, as well. The more interconnected and faster your system, the more it becomes unstable. The more your system is unstable, the more the governance is challenging. Besides, every one of you has clearly in mind the fact of the speed of evolution of IT, but if you look at this fact from another point of view it means that everything in IT is becoming obsolete very, very fast. If you compare your work with the work of our counterparts in other departments, we can say that none of us has the full control over what his professionals are doing. If after 2 years you are not working on new technology, you are obsolete. The only thing you can do is to build strong professional relationships to guide our team, not to 'master and commander' them. I personally would not be able to follow up a deep technical discussion with my system administrator on operating systems hardening for no more than ten minutes before I get lost. You are younger, so maybe you could last 30 minutes, but I am quite sure your best system administrator has a vertical knowledge you do not master any more. You cannot help but trust him; there is no other way to manage the complexity. And I hope you made the right choice! This is different, for example, from what is happening to my counterpart in administration: no one of his collaborators knows more than he knows. He is a manager who performed all the jobs in his team and the competencies required are not much different now than 20 years ago. In our field, the fact that somebody was able to work on operating systems 20 years ago means nothing for today IT context.

"The second point is about boundaries. What is really in the scope of IT management and governance? What is under the responsibility of a CIO and what is out of scope for him? And above all, who is in charge of what is outside the borders of a CIO's kingdom? Nowadays ICT is practically everywhere. IT is managing not only information but production processes as well: alarm systems, building automation, diagnostic equipment. Yes, because speaking of our context, you know well that clinical engineering management is an issue: once they were stand-alone equipment with minimal embedded software; now they are often complex client server systems, most of the time outside the CIO's span of control and managed by clinical engineers. And clinical engineers do not always have the proper background to manage the IT side of the equipment, without speaking of complex architectural and security issues.

"The third point is linked to the perception users have of IT. I remind myself often of two extreme points of view in which many of the users are represented. The first one is what I call the 'Harry Potter Syndrome.' I got the name from the main character of the famous saga and from an episode that happened to me when I was a young CIO. I was starting to work in a complex environment and I spent the first 6 months meeting people and trying to understand the best strategy to get out of the mess. One day I met a user in a suburban clinic who told me, 'So you are the new Harry Potter! Make sure you have the right wand to solve all of our problems!' This point of view is what I call 'Informagic': the magic solution to all the problems. In fact, in the Harry Potter saga, technology to humans was equivalent to magic for wizards. The second attitude I often find in IT users is what I call the 'waste collection syndrome.' I'm taking it from another user who, during a customer satisfaction survey on IT department, wrote, 'IT should be like waste collection: you should work in the shadows, early in the morning, clean up everything and let us work in peace.'

Here he stopped for a while. He was not using slides; he did not need them. Every single person was totally focused on his speech. He went on, "As you can understand, both the extremes are misleading. In the first case we are asking IT to do what it cannot possibly do. To solve complex problems requires a clear definition of objectives and a mix of technology, organization and process review. In the other case the user is dreaming of an IT "behind the scenes", loosely interacting with people and processes. This is impossible as well, since we are strongly bonded to processes and organization.

"And this is the fourth and last point: the interconnection between IT, processes and organization. We could argue IT is like the 'secret ingredient' of many recipes. We could also say IT is indispensable in many recipes. But it cannot be the only one. IT could be the salt or the yeast. But you cannot compensate for a lack of flour by using more yeast, and you cannot make a good soup using more salt than other ingredients. Unfortunately, I have seen this happen many times in the last years.

"In summary, for the four reasons I just told you and for many others you could think of, the traditional CIO is not enough anymore. And I am conscious I am saying that while we are still struggling to develop CIOs from IT Managers. But CIO is still not enough. In some companies you can find the CISO, Chief Information and Security Officer, but this is not enough either. I could tell you I had a dream. And in my dream there were many more letters between the C and the O than a miserable I. In my dream, there was something like a Chief of Holistic Information, Automation and Risk Information Systems and Security Implementation and Management Officer." While he was saying that, he wrote on an electronic dashboard: C.H.I.A.R.I.S.S.I.M.O.

"Is it too much? Too long as a title? Can you imagine your CEO if every time he has to introduce you during a meeting he has to say, 'This is Jim Smith, my C.H.I.A.R.I.S.S.I.M.O.,' spelling each letter?" You could hear the participants laughing by now. "Yes, a little longer than usual indeed, but I can tell you that in reality there is much more than what I included in the title, as in the full word there is more than what you can find in any single letter. Because I firmly believe that communications skills will be of paramount importance now and in the future. And CHIARISSIMO, in the beautiful language which is Italian, as far as I can remember, means not only an honorific title but is also the superlative of CHIARO. Tommaso is from Rome and can confirm that. Chiaro means clear, transparent, comprehensible to everybody, as the communication of our guy should be. He should have a holistic approach to technology, and he needs to be a primary actor of enterprise risk management, since I can bet risks will be more and more linked to IT. Now you certainly did not miss a negligible detail: if it is difficult to find someone with the right mix of skills and competencies to be a good CIO, who could possibly manage to be a good CHIARISSIMO? Can a single man, as able and prepared as you could imagine, handle so

many different fields, ranging from applications to regulations, from enabling technologies to processes and security, from automation and risk management, and still be able to act as a strategist, an architect and a communicator? Or are we drawing a kind of superhero only Marvel could create?
Or shouldn't we instead completely change our mental paradigm, trying to delegate responsibilities and creating, for example, a C.I.A.O.S, a Chief of Information and Automation Officer and Strategist able to govern strategies and architectures and using executive level coworkers to govern information, processes and technologies?" While Martin paused for effect Hannah, the GHISA secretary, entered the room. Excusing herself and quite embarrassed, she handed over an urgent message for Martin from his Chief Technology Officer and vice CIO Mark Swan. Martin was really puzzled. In 30 years of his career he had never been interrupted during a lesson. He read the message and his astonished students saw him growing gloomy. In fact the message read:

Martin,
Sorry to disturb you during your lesson but we just declared the state of crisis at level 3, as the emergency procedure prescribes. In fact, one hour and a half ago we discovered a data security breach on the main data center which impacted our hospital. We experienced anomalies with high risk for patients on CT Scans and NMRs. I tried to contact you immediately but without success, so I decided to declare the state of crisis myself. After a preliminary analysis, the situation looked so serious we started the controlled shut down procedure of all systems and the activation of the disaster recovery data center. Now the secondary data center is active and the situation seems under control, at least for the IT department. I have no clear information from our Clinical Engineering colleagues. The cloud-based collaboration systems never stopped working and they were a precious tool to keep the users, the colleagues and the executives updated and to avoid panic. Users experienced less than one hour downtime and now all the systems are operating at

90% level. We activated the perimeter protection procedure and we closed all the accesses non-essential to core systems.

One last point: from my informal contacts, it seems we are not the only hospital under attack: the situation is quite serious in town.

Please call me back as soon as you read this message.

Mark

Martin stopped for a while, thinking, then said, "Hannah, please immediately summon an emergency meeting. I want the CIOs of the hospitals in town connected via video conference within 45 minutes. If possible ask them to come here physically. And I want someone from CIRANO with us! And now please put me in touch with Mark Swan on the cell phone and try to contact Ned Wal, as well."

Then he turned to his bewildered audience and said, "My dear students, today we stop here. It seems we will have an interesting case study on IT security and business continuity for the next lesson!"

Chapter 18. Emergency Meeting. Location: Canada, GHISA training center. Timeline: present time, April 16, 10:30 a.m.

After he spoke to Marc on the phone, Martin was even more worried, but not for his hospital. Luckily in the last years, thanks to a good dialog with the CEO, Martin and his team were able to build a resilient infrastructure, robust and reasonably safe. The reaction to the attack of the morning was a demonstration of this: without him being present, all the safety procedures were put into operation properly and service disruptions had been, considering the magnitude of the problem, restrained.

Even the use of clout services, a topic quite disputed in the last period and on which Martin always tried to have a pragmatic and thoughtful approach, had been strategically important to keep open the communications among the users during the critical phase of systems downtime. Thinking about it, Martin felt quite proud of the work his team had performed in the past years. Unfortunately he was well aware that, in spite of the efforts of Martin and other CIOs, at group level the security strategy had not always been very well-judged. Ned Wal was very sensitive to security risks and a champion of cautious use of technology, but often it seemed he did not frame this sensitivity in a system or architectural framework—or at least he was never able to promote this kind of approach with group CEO.

Besides that, three things were bothering Martin now. The first one was related to "boundaries." It was one of the topics of his lesson and one of the worries of his professional life.
However high his reputation, however wide his leadership inside and outside the IT field, getting him as far as to be elected Vice President with focus on Process Improvements, he was never able to convince the hospital management to include diagnostic and medical equipment in his scope of action. Everyone in his hospital knew well that the Clinical Engineering team had the core competencies to handle the devices but not the information technology side of the medical equipment. From what he understood from Marc's report, though he did not have hard facts

The Fifth Domain - 91

about it, in Clinical Engineering they experienced serious breakdowns.

The second thought that was troubling him was that, as his connections in other hospitals confirmed, there were at least 4 more hospitals in town under attack which were really having hard times. The third worry was that Ned Wal could not be reached in the past 10 days. Knowing Ned, this was really peculiar. Adding to this the strange e-mails Tommaso was telling him about a few days before, the picture was quite gloomy.

By now all the participants to the call were connected. Besides him, only two CIOs of the 7 hospital CIOs in town were physically present. The other 4 were connected, expressing the need for their presence in their hospital in that difficult moment. This was a clear indicator of a crisis underway.

They were about to start when the video conference system announced a new participant, a tiny girl with very short hair. She looked more like a teenager, out of place in that meeting of IT managers, all men and all above 40 years old. She introduced herself as Diana Simpson, special agent of Canadian CIRANO. Martin had heard about her and if she was worth just the half of what he thought, well, she was welcome!

After a few minutes for the regular greetings, Martin went straight to the point. Helped by Marc, connected in video conference, he depicted the situation in his hospital and asked the other CIOs to update the other meeting participants on the situations in theirs.

The picture was bewildering. All the other 6 CIOs declared they were under attack. Five of the seven hospitals in town were part of the TotalHealth Group. The other two were not part of TotalHealth but they were still connected in the same regional health care network, an extranet which had probably been a medium for the spreading of contagion.

The outcomes of the attacks had been quite different, with a scale ranging from serious to devastating. This was a demonstration, Martin thought, of how vulnerable our systems are and how vital information systems were for hospitals' operations. In fact, Martin's hospital was the only one operating almost at full capacity. The others were functioning at 20% or 30% at the best: they reverted many services to manual, but this was slowing down everything so much they had to send back patients. Laboratory and imaging were fundamentally blocked, operating theatres and emergency departments slowed down dramatically: a delirium.

In two hospitals, including his, 3 patients undertaking a CAT and one exposed to NMR were under clinical observation since the attack caused a malfunction of the diagnostic equipment control systems. Patients were exposed to a X-rays and magnetic field levels completely out of range. In at least one case the level of radiation was so high as to put the patient's life in danger. In one hospital the NMR was activated during the maintenance operations: the 3 TESLA magnetic field threw a cylinder and some tools at the maintenance team, wounding some of them.

At this point, CIRANO's agent, silent up to that moment, intervened. She cleared her throat, as a shy teenager speaking to adults, but when she started speaking her determination and interior strength were evident in every word she said, "At CIRANO we have reasons to think we are witnessing a massive cyber-attack prepared a long time ago. We are in touch with IT security agencies in other countries and with the national and international police organizations. Unfortunately our information was fragmented and inconsistent and up to now it was not possible to anticipate where the attack would strike. Now we know. We have reason to think, based on a conversation I had with him one month ago, that Ned Wal was on the track of something. Unfortunately, he disappeared. Last time he was seen in Kiev. The local police and Interpol are looking for him. If you should have any relevant information about him please contact me immediately."

She was going close the channel, when Martin added, "I think the last person in TotalHealth who spoke to Ned was Tommaso Degregori, a colleague from Rome. He received strange e-mails from Ned, as well. I think you might be interested to have a chat with Degregori: I am not sure, but maybe Ned left some 'clues.'"

Diana looked at him straight and said simply, "Mr. Hunter, I'm waiting for you tomorrow morning at 10 a.m. in CIRANO headquarters. I'll ensure that Degregori will be there as well."

Chapter 19. Safe house. Location: Castelli Romani. Timeline: present time, April 16, 20:45 a.m.

Tommaso's travel was quite tormented. He got no answers to his questions and he was asked not to contact anybody. They arrived in a lonely mansion on the lake of Albano, close to Castel Gandolfo, the summer residence of the Popes. Tommaso and Myriam always liked the area of Castelli Romani: to them it was a peaceful retreat when they could not take any more of the chaos of Rome.

It was a landscape of hills, fortified citadels and volcanic lakes. Just a few knew that it was the area of the big Volcano Laziale, a still-active immense volcano which could in the future wake up again.

As they passed the gate of the park the cars stopped. Tommaso got out of the car with a jump as he saw Myriam on the entrance of the villa waiting for him. They embraced for a long time quietly. Then Myriam, with watery eyes, said, "What's going on Tommaso?"

He hugged her some more, then he said, "I am not sure, I only got fragments of information, but I do believe it has something to do with what I told you about Ned, remember?" She nodded silently, but they could not say much more because another car arrived.

A man in his forties got out and introduced himself as Inspector Davide Bernasconi from Interpol. He invited them to come in and, while they were sitting in the kitchen, he explained what he could, "Sorry for the inconvenience, but first of all I want you to know you are safe here. We had to intervene urgently because it seems a massive cyber-attack on TotalHealth clinics in Canada is underway. It seems Ned Wal — that you, Mr. Degregori, know well — disappeared after he discovered some important clues. We think everyone who got in touch with him in the last days could be on one side a source of precious information, but on the other side could be the target of whoever kidnapped Wal."

Tommaso sat for a while deep in thought, then said, "So what are you planning, to keep us here forever?"

The inspector was unimpressed, "Not at all. Your wife will stay here for a while; you will leave on a military plane tomorrow morning at 5 a.m. from the military airport of Ciampino."

"And where am I supposed to go, if I may ask?"

"To Canada, of course, but I cannot reveal more," the inspector answered.

They were escorted to the master bedroom with a massive bed coming probably from the end of the 19th century, as were the other pieces of furniture, which put them quite in awe. The bodyguards set themselves at ground floor. Myriam and Tommaso did not speak much; they had not much more information to share that what they heard. Tommaso could not help noticing ISAHBeL. "I see you did not come alone."

She answered, "Yes, of course, otherwise who will wake me up in the morning now that you will abandon me? Jokes aside, we are out of town and I am pregnant: to have ISAHBeL close to me makes me feel safer."

He smiled but did not say anything. When they were in bed, he shared with her the thoughts about the last year's episodes he was having during his car trip. She just asked, "Are you going to be away for long?"

He reassured her he really did not have much information to share, so probably they would send him back home soon. She kissed him and turned on her side. He embraced her and they spent the night like that, in the position they called "spoon and fork", with his hand on her womb, but neither of them could really sleep much.

Chapter 20. Unexpected departure. Location: military airport of Ciampino (Rome). Timeline: present time, April 17, 4:45 a.m.

The travel from the safe house to the military airport of Ciampino was quite short, since the lake of Albano was not far from the airport. Tommaso could not stop visualizing Myriam hugging him while she was crying silently. He tried to reassure her, but to be honest he was quite uneasy himself: for all what he knew, he could be away one day or one month.

Tommaso got in the military airplane waiting for him on the airport runway with engines ready and bodyguards waiting for him. He was fastening his seatbelt when somebody else boarded. Tommaso remained speechless, but there was no doubt: it was Aaron! Tommaso unfastened his belt and ran to greet him. Aaron was confused and upset, with the face of somebody who had not slept in the past two days. "Aaron, I must admit you caught me by surprise! What the hell are you doing here?"

Aaron smiled faintly. They sat down side by side and he started to say, "I was not able to get in touch with Sheila in the past three days. You know recently she has been away quite a lot, but we are constantly in touch at least once a day via social networks. I thought she was not well, so I tried to contact her on the phone and ... a lady answered on the phone. She was speaking in English — Canadian accent, I would say. I thought she was a friend of Sheila. She stayed with me on the phone for a while, asking me a number of questions, and at the end she said Sheila had been arrested and she was an agent of Canadian Police. At that point I hung up, but no less than one hour after the call these kind gentlemen were in front of my door and they asked me to follow them. I did not understand much, but I figure it out that during her interrogation she gave them my name."

Tommaso was able to hold back his thoughts about social networks and dangerous friendships coming out of the net. More pieces of the puzzle were fitting together. He simply said, "Well, let's enjoy this trip to Canada: I think we will find it interesting what we will discover!"

Chapter 21. A crucial track. Location: Canada, CIRANO Headquarters. Timeline: present time, April 17, 10:00 a.m. local time

Diana kept her word, but Martin never doubted it. As promised, in the Canadian CIRANO Headquarter, besides him, Diana and a couple of her team members, he met Tommaso as well. They greeted warmly. Diana was also able to locate Fred, the security consultant of TotalHealth group and one of the closest of Ned's collaborators, and Aaron, a system administrator of Tommaso's team. Tommaso and Aaron's faces spoke of a sleepless night but this was understandable, thinking about the different time zones and the fact that, to be there at lunch time, they probably left Italy before dawn.

Diana didn't like to waste time. She summarized the situation shortly, since each one of them had knowledge only of a part of the mosaic and nobody, not ever herself, could have the full picture. "Dear sirs, I invited you to join our team because the situation is serious and each one of you probably has fragments of relevant information. I'll try to sum it up to everyone's benefit.

In the last months the IT security agencies of the major industrialized countries have been monitoring abnormal activities on the 'net from the most important cyber-criminals. No need to give you more details, but you probably know we have quite a number of undercover agents in the most important illegal websites used by criminals to buy and sell credit card numbers, access credentials to the various IT systems and personal information as well. In the last period we noticed the transactions intensifying, even if the most important messages were encrypted, so we could not understand them. We were waiting to understand what would have been the objective of all this fuss and from yesterday we know: we are experiencing a massive cyber-attack. The epicenter seems to be TotalHealth and specifically the town where its headquarters are located in Canada. Since yesterday all the hospitals in town are under attack. It seems the attackers were able to break both TotalHealth security measures and the security of the Health Care Regional network connecting all the hospitals.

The Fifth Domain - 98

The damages to information systems in six hospitals out of seven were so intensive they have been forced to revert to manual procedures for patient management. You know better than I do what this means: it's like the attackers destroyed 5 hospitals out of 7, since 6 of them are actually operating at no more the 20% of their capacity and the one better in shape is only operating at 80-90% of his capacity. Moreover, the attack was designed to damage the control systems of medical and diagnostic equipment as well. We ended up with a patient entering the hospital for a CAT and coming out like he did a stroll in Fukushima. Other patients were exposed to abnormal magnetic fields and do not ask me what consequences this will have on them. Maybe it is better not to know. In another case a NMR was turned on during maintenance operations. Results: metallic objects flying like bullets and two of the maintenance crew wounded. Nice outcome for a few hours of battle. We do not know if this is the end or the beginning of the attack and have no specific clues, but the evidence we collected leads us to think your input will be vital.

"First evidence: we arrested a girl who had been in touch with Mr. Aaron here. She called herself Sheila. You can see her picture on the screens." And Sheila showed up on the big screen and in the smaller ones around the room, in a picture taken on a beach. Looking at the picture Tommaso could not help thinking the he could understand why Aaron lost his head over her. With one eye he noticed Aaron's sorry and worried expression, but he did not say a word.

Diana went on, "Sheila was in Malta with a man, probably a key player among the criminals we are chasing, but he was able to escape." Aaron lowered his head. "At this very moment Sheila is under examination but up to now we could not get much from her. We just know she is from Ukraine, she has questionable acquaintances and she has been often in Rome in the last year. I think I do not need to add more." Icy pause, total silence. "Second evidence: Ned Wal probably discovered something, but he disappeared before he could feed us more information. Any single piece of news about Ned is valuable to us. That's all for me; now we would like to listen to you."

The situation was quite embarrassing for Aaron, who did not speak a word. Tommaso thought it was too much for Aaron and decided to move on giving his contribution, "A few days ago Ned sent me two peculiar e-mails."

Diana raised an eyebrow and asked, "Can we see them?"

Tommaso had still the printed copy in his pocket, he did not know if by chance or by intuition. He put them on the table. Diana was reading them aloud and paused for a while. One of her collaborators asked, "Should I summon someone from the Encryption department?" Diana thought for a while, then she said, "No need. The code is trivial. A kid could have deciphered it." Tommaso sighed: that woman had the touch of an elephant. She took a red marker and, counting the words, looped three numbers and three words. Then she put the printed e-mail in the middle of the table.

FIRST MAIL (from Ned's company e-mail to Tommaso's company e-mail):
April 6 -time: 11:34 a.m.
from: Ned Wal
to: Tommaso Degregori

Subject: Telephone number

Dear Tom,
here is the phone number you were asking me last week:
(+39) 2 58 80
Best regards
Ned

PS: next time I'll be back to the Headquarters, I'll remove the encryption from my laptop. I think it is slowing down the processor too much ...

SECOND MAIL (from Ned's personal e-mail to Tommaso's personal e-mail):
April 6 - time: 11:34 a.m.
from: Ned Wal
to: Tommaso Degregori

Subject: Social Networks

Dear Tom,
I have been thinking a lot about social networks in the past week. You know, I told you once that you fly too high on some topics, and this is probably one of those. But, considering better the evolution of the society, I think we should venture more in experimenting the power of social networks. You could be a pioneer with your group. Don't be amazed by my new attitude on the subject: old people sometimes are fools, sometimes are wise ... Besides, you know, I discovered that social networks are extremely useful if you want to know better somebody. There are so many information about all of us out there I could hardly imagine before. My greetings to your wonderful wife Myriam.

See you soon
Ned

"The encryption algorithm is based on words' position in text: the telephone number identifies the position of the relevant words in the second e-mail. In fact, in the first e-mail Ned is speaking of encryption. It's a clue: Ned used a simple code hoping you would be able to understand it by yourself. Maybe he overestimated you. Anyway, he did not trust to use explicit messages or keywords in the e-mail and this means he suspected to be tracked. What I do not understand, however, is the key of the message. It looks like a generic warning. The three words compose the sentence: 'Fly you fools'. I would expect something more from Ned."

Now Aaron spoke out, "I believe there is more. In the second e-mail there is a clue. I suppose ... I mean, I am not sure but it is possible that Sheila used our relationship ... to collect information about me in order to gain access to my system administrator passwords." Then he explained the basic rule he used in forming his passwords.

Fred added sadly, "What else can be said? With the basic rule ... anything else they needed is public on your social networks profiles. This was what Ned meant. And with your level of authorization ... it was a kid's game to enter the main data center and to violate the systems."

Here it was Diana's turn to signal everybody to stop, since she caught an enlightenment in Tommaso's face. After a moment Tommaso said, "The sentence. At the beginning I did not recognize it since I remembered it in Italian. It is not a generic warning. It is a quotation, even if I do not understand fully what he meant. It comes from 'The Lord of the Rings', one of Ned's favorite books. 'Fly you fools' is what Gandalf is shouting to his friends before being drowned in the abyss by the Balrog ... 'Fuggite sciocchi' in Italian."

Here Tommaso paused, since Diana literally jumped out of her seat and ordered her coworkers, "Follow me, now!" and they were gone.

Chapter 22. Interrogatory. Location: Canada, CIRANO Headquarters. Timeline: present time, April 17, 9:30 p.m. local time

Diana came back in the meeting room after a few hours' leave with the two assistants following her. In the meantime they broke their fast with a frugal dinner and they were shown a room with a few camp beds. It was clear the night would be long.

As usual Diana was leading the situation and she updated them about what happened during the past hours, "We spent the afternoon sieving the communications of the last months in cyber-criminality underworld. There was a keyword missing to discriminate what was related to the ongoing attack and what was actually pure entropy or business as usual. Wal gave us the key: it seems the current raid is called "Operation Balrog." Don't ask me why, I do not know and I am not so interested in discovering it. The world is full of psychopaths and literature lovers. Some are both. I am neither of the two. However, searching back through the relevant communications of the last months, we were able to piece together part of the plan. First of all, the attack is in 3 waves. Yesterday we experienced the first wave. We were not able to prevent it; we can just try to repair the damage. We will probably need a week's work. The second wave had telecommunication and energy distribution systems as targets. I said 'had' because this time we were able to prevent it. We have been in touch with the most important telephone operators and energy companies since 4 p.m. and it seems our countermeasures are quite effective. We had a few problems on intercontinental calls, but the basic infrastructure is operating normally. Energy distribution had no impact at all."

Tommaso could not restrain his curiosity, "And what and when will be the third wave?"

Diana looked down at him as if he was a dumb schoolboy and answered with too much of an educational style for Tommaso's taste, "If I knew the answer, I would not be here wasting my time with you. We do not know much about the third wave. We just know it will come, but we have no clues on the timing and the target. Of course all the critical systems, from energy to banking to telecommunication and health care, have been alerted. But the possibilities are virtually infinite. The only foothold we have is the girl with whom Mr. Aaron started such a close friendship."

Aaron was not looking at her and he remained head down. Tommaso was thinking, *I must correct myself. I can see the limits of my analogy between her and an elephant. I am not sure, but her empathy level reminds me better of someone like Jack the Ripper.*

Diana continued, "I do believe it is better for you to attend the interrogation. You can follow it from a closed room looking at the camera images. You help us to evaluate the information we will get from her."

Half an hour later they were in the interrogation wing of the building. Tommaso did not expect to find it in CIRANO headquarters, but apparently it could be useful sometimes. From the screens they could see Sheila entering a room where a woman agent was waiting for her. Sheila looked as beautiful as ever but she was clearly afraid and she probably did not sleep much in the past days. The agent was kind; she raised her voice only once. Aaron got up from his chair to ease the tension. Tommaso thought all this was probably torture to him. She was probably the first girl he fell in love with. The interrogation went on for an hour before Sheila could really give any useful piece of information: they could not decide whether she was a skilled professional or a useless pawn who did not know anything. Then around 11 p.m. something happened. Sheila started to sweat profusely. She got up, shouting she was not feeling well, she had pain in all her body. The agent initially shouted back at her, then tried to calm her down. Aaron was looking at Tommaso and the others more nervously every minute. A second later the agent was shouting at the phone, "A doctor please, we have an emergency."

They could see Sheila falling backward before the images went off, while Aaron was shouting himself, "She is sick, she has diabetes! Help her!"

Chapter 23. Night. Location: Canada, CIRANO Headquarters. Timeline: present time, April 18, 1:30 a.m. local time

After the tragic interrogation of the previous evening, they were all very shaken. They were informed that Sheila was now in the hospital in serious condition. Aaron was shocked. They reached their sleeping room with the camp beds. Tommaso tried to get in touch with Myriam by phone but, probably as a consequence of the attack, it was not possible. Fortunately she was online in her TotalPersonalProfile account and they were able to exchange a few messages. She was OK; after all, the safe house was in a wonderful position. She informed her co-workers she was taking a few days off. The bodyguards were very kind and she did not miss anything but Tommaso's presence. He updated her about the last events and about Sheila. Despite the coldness of the communication media used, he could almost feel her empathy and proximity. As was her nature, she urged him to go offline and to comfort Aaron, who was, in a way, like an adopted son for her. It was typical of Myriam to sacrifice the few moments she could have with Tommaso in order to help someone in need. They greeted warmly, at least as warmly as the medium allowed them, and Tommaso went for Aaron. He was curled up in his bed. He did not want to speak. Tommaso lay down in the closest camp bed, but he could not do much other than try to sleep a little to recover his strength.

Chapter 24. Sheila. Location: Canada, CIRANO Headquarters. Timeline: present time, April 18, 6:30 a.m. local time

Tommaso was dreaming of Myriam: she was waking him up with a kiss, as she often did when they were at home together. She moved her body on top of him, pushed away his hair and kissed him softly on his forehead. He could almost smell her scent, he could feel her thin silky nightgown and he was going, as usual, to embrace her hips and to kiss gently her lips ... when Diana entered, slamming the door and urging everybody to get ready immediately: she would be waiting for them in the meeting room in 15 minutes. Now Tommaso was back to reality, not much rested by the night and hating the woman who departed him from Myriam so abruptly. But when he turned to Aaron and saw his face, the face of someone who did not sleep at all, his rage disappeared. Maybe Jack the Ripper did not sleep either, but she did not show up any signs of weariness at all. When they were all in the meeting room, Diana told them (showing for the first time a sign of humanity) she was sorry to communicate that Sheila died that very night in the hospital. An autopsy would probably clarify the cause of death. Unfortunately, they could not stop here because they were receiving abnormal reports from the city hospitals. Since the previous evening, the number of heart attacks was oddly high compared with the statistics they had. City hospitals were distributing defibrillators in key points in the city. It was not clear if the peak could simply be explained with the current crisis and the subsequent state of alert of the population, who has been informed by the communication media both on the situation and on the hospitals' limited capacity to handle critical patients, or if the cause could be another. She did not say more, but there was a hint of concern in all their eyes.

Chapter 25. The third wave. Location: Canada, CIRANO Headquarters. Timeline: present time, April 18, 9:30 a.m. local time

At 9:30 a.m., after scarce and incongruous news, Diana's boss Thomas entered the room. He introduced himself shortly and greeted everybody genially. Tommaso felt sorry for him, who had the burden to manage a coworker as Diana, but obviously didn't say a word about it.

Thomas was bringing them fresh news, unfortunately not good. First of all they received the results of the autopsy on Sheila. The death was caused by a malfunctioning implanted insulin pump Sheila had in her abdomen. In a few seconds all the insulin needed for one month was released.

Tommaso looked at Aaron quizzically and he said, "Yes, I told you she had diabetes. Recently she decided to have a device implanted."

Tommaso had no time to ask who produced the device, since Thomas added, "I believe there is a worse piece of news on the TV right now you should know about. There is a press conference ongoing with the CEO of IMD. Diana, please …"

On the big screens of the meeting room the CEO appeared. He had the embarrassed and contrite look CEOs have when they are going to disclose something that will surely affect the share price of their company. You could read in his face something like, "If I were Japanese, I would commit Hara-kiri now." When he spoke, Tommaso heard him saying what he was afraid of, "After careful evaluation of the events of the last hours on some of the patients using our implantable devices and after thorough analysis by our best engineers, we discovered a potential security problem on our devices. An update is ready to upgrade the control software of our devices. The devices will be updated without any surgery since, as you know, our technology allows us to update our devices via wireless connections. We ask all the patients carrying an IMD pacemaker or insulin pump, as a precautionary measure, to switch off the monitoring station ISAHBeL and to reach as soon as possible the closest hospital qualified to work on our technology. We thank you all and we assure you everything will be done to minimize the nuisances of such an operation. Thanks."

Thomas closed the connection and added, "We have reasons to believe this is the third wave. The 'nuisances' he was speaking about means the 12 people who died between yesterday night and this morning. We are not sure all of the death are related to IMD, since we are still …"

But he could not finish the sentence: Tommaso jumped out of his chair and ran out of the room with his cell phone in his hand.

Martin explained, "His wife, Myriam, has had an IMD pacemaker since 4 years ago …"

Chapter 26. Myriam. Location: Canada, CIRANO Headquarters. Timeline: present time, April 18, 10:30 p.m. local time

Tommaso was trying unsuccessfully to get in touch with Myriam. Now he came back to the meeting room and was sitting, holding his head in his hands. Every thirty seconds he tried to call again. Suddenly he was aware that a small hand was on his shoulder. When he raised his eyes he saw Diana, who said, "We were able to get in touch with the operating center in Rome. Unfortunately, they were not able to get in touch with your wife's bodyguards. Two helicopters took off from Rome a few minutes ago, with a crew of special forces and medical doctors, including an IMD engineer. They are trained to handle both a medical emergency and a violation of the perimeter of the safe house. We cannot do anything but wait."

Tommaso nodded and mechanically re-dialed Myriam's number for the hundredth time, but again nobody answered.

Chapter 27. Kernel Software System Update – Critical 0-days patch n. 100813MEN-PASS. Location: surrounding of Rome. Timeline: present time, April 18, 11:30 p.m. local time

Tommaso was sitting in the corridor close to the meeting room. Diana arrived and handed him a wireless phone without speaking. At the other end of the line Myriam's warm voice said, "You had better send me some flowers."

Tommaso was confused and elated at the same time. He answered like an idiot, "What? Are you OK? What happened?"

She answered, as calm as usual, "I was saying, if you wanted me to notice how much do you care for me, you had better send me some flowers with a note card. Anyway, yes, I am fine. But you should have seen the show."

"What show?" he asked, quite curious by now.

"The show of my rescue. Today in late afternoon I was able to convince — and I admit now it wasn't a particularly good idea — my bodyguards to let me have a short hike along the lake. There is a nice trail, you know. They allowed my walk only with the condition they would follow me all the time. So there I was, hiking with 4 bodyguards behind me, just like Lady Di in her best times. Along the trail there are quite a few dead spots for the cell phones and we went through one of these spots, so I did not receive your calls. We were going back to our safe house when my bodyguard received a call on their radios. The tone was nervous, so obviously something was going wrong, but they did not tell me anything. We just stopped there. They prepared to 'defend the perimeter' — at least, so they said. After a few minutes we saw two black military helicopters flying close to the water, followed by a police motorboat at maximum speed. The helicopters stopped above us and three commandos from each helicopter, plus a stretcher, descended from ropes — you know, like you see in the movies. In the meantime the policemen jumped from the motorboat and took up position on the beach. Two of the commandos talked to my bodyguards, the other four came toward me and two of them threw me down in the stretcher. Another one was holding one of the devices they used during our check-up for the pacemaker and the last one was just there over me with a defibrillator ready to be used! I shouted at him, 'Stop it, I am pregnant!' Only then he put down the defibrillator. If I did not die there, I'll probably never die!"

Tommaso was smiling now, but he asked promptly, "And where are you now?"

"Now I am in a military hospital. After they got me on the helicopter, fastened to the stretcher, they brought me here, where they performed what the IMD engineer called in his report a 'Kernel Software System Update – Critical 0-days patch n. 100813MEN-PASS.' Then he added smoothly, 'Dear lady, now your software is updated and faultlessly working.'"

Tommaso could not help laughing now. Myriam was laughing as well, unlike in the last weeks. He concluded, "You know, last time a witnessed an operation of the like was a critical 0 days path installed by Aaron on the e-mail server of the hospital. But it was not nearly so dramatic and the update introduced new pernicious bugs which required a subsequent update to be resolved.

"Yes," she added, "so now you know that if I start behaving oddly it's a side effect of the '0-days patch n. 100813MEN-PASS'." They laughed again, a cathartic laugh, then Myriam added, "My dear, I need to leave you now, they are bringing me back to the safe house. But you do not need to worry: a cardiologist will be with me all the time and I turned off ISAHBeL. Bye and … next time remember: just send me some flowers!"

So they parted, and Tommaso's heart began to beat normally again.

When he raised his head, he saw Diana looking at him with a non-belligerent look. It was probably the 'maximum empathy level' she was designed for. He overcame his instinctive aversion for the woman and said, "Thank you."

She was already turning her back to him when she answered, "It is my duty, Degregori, just my duty. Now please, I need to ask you to come in again. The situation is escalating."

Chapter 28. Exodus. Location: Canada, CIRANO Headquarters. Timeline: present time, April 18, 12:00 p.m. (noon) local time

The announcement by the IMD CEO started a panic among the patients with an IMD implantable device. Unfortunately, in the town where the headquarters of TotalHealth and IMD were, the still ongoing cyber-attack and the panic caused by the IMD CEO's announcement generated a multiplier effect, since the hospitals were still, speaking of IT systems, a pile of rubble.

If the first news were true, of the 12 cases of heart attack, 9 were IMD patients living in town. The other 3 were patients living in other countries, but after a careful analysis 2 of them turned out to be a false alarm, and one was still under investigation. In another case a patient, after a wrong glycaemia test performed by ISAHBeL, inoculated himself with an insulin dose double that needed and ended up in a hospital. The 9 deaths of IMD patients were all due to a cardiac arrest apparently caused by an anomaly in the electric signal the pacemaker was sending to the heart to set the pace of the heartbeat. They did not reach the hospitals alive. By now all the patients with IMD devices were rushing to the nearest hospital. This was the straw that broke the camel's back. Martin's hospital, the only one functioning almost wholly, become the healthcare hub for the emergencies. They activated the Emergency Operations Plan and the Incident Command System, but this was not enough: the mayor decided to surrender and ordered a one-week temporary evacuation of the town.

Chapter 29. The White. Location: Canada, CIRANO Headquarters. Timeline: present time, April 18, 2:30 p.m. local time

Tommaso was reading two e-mails he just received:

MAIL 1 (from Ned's company e-mail to Tommaso's company e-mail):
Ore: 14:13
from: Ian McKellen
to: Tommaso Degregori

Subject: Telephone number

Dear Tommaso
Here is the telephone number I strongly suggest you to call: (+ 380 (0)482) 35 66 86
Ian

MAIL 2 (from Ned's personal e-mail to Tommaso's personal e-mail):
Ore: 14:13
from: Ian McKellen
to: Tommaso Degregori

Subject: Contact

Dear Tommaso,
Probably you do not remember me, but we met at the last GHISA convention. I was sitting by your side during the last day. I had you on my left side and Wal on my right side. We had little time to talk, but I was very impressed by your speech. As you probably know, I am currently the CTO of one of the TotalHealth Hospitals in the north-east of Europe. I like my job, but my family is tired of living here. White and snow for 6-7 months a year! I am currently evaluating alternatives to my current position. I was in Rome with

my family one year ago and we enjoyed Italy so much! Please consider me if you see any opening in Italy for a CTO or CIO position.

Ciao e grazie di tutto!

Ian

Tommaso read the e-mail with the hope rising in his heart, recognizing the style. There was no need of recalling he had never been at the last GHISA convention and that Ian McKellen was the actor interpreting Gandalf in Peter Jackson's movies. This time he deciphered the message quickly and smiled:

word n. 35: Wal
word n. 61: the
word n. 86: White.

"Wal the White." Now he was sure: as Gandalf after fighting with the Balrog returns from death as "Gandalf the White", so Wal was well alive and was coming back … He hurried back to the meeting room where Diana and the others were eating a frugal meal. From his look they understood at once that good news arrived at last. He showed them the e-mails and added triumphantly to Diana, "Wal is alive!"

Diana studied the e-mails for a while and said plainly, "Yes, and he told us where to find him as well." Tommaso's dumb look allowed Diana to added didactically, "Yes, Mr. Degregori, you should pay more attention to the details. I bet the telephone number this time is real. But do not feel let down; you must be trained to read the clues. The international prefix is from Ukraine and the local prefix identifies Odessa. I know it because for us working with cyber-criminals, Odessa is the crossroad of the worst of this world. And in the first e-mail Ian/Wal is saying: 'Here is the telephone number I strongly suggest you call'. A different expression from what he used before and much more explicit. So let's try to connect with this number."

Chapter 30. Shakil. Location: Canada-Odessa. Timeline: present time, April 18, 3:00 p.m. local time

Tommaso, Martin, Aaron, Fred and Diana with her assistants were in the meeting room. Aaron was still shocked: after Sheila died he did not say a word. They were calling the Odessa telephone number. After three rings, Wal's voice erupted, as vigorous as usual, "Damn, you took your time! Tom, I thought you were more skilled in deciphering my messages."

Diana could not help saying, "Well, don't blame him; he just needed some help. I am Special Agent Diana Simpson from the Canadian CIRANO. We are calling you from our operating center, where we are trying to limit the damage of the crisis."

Wal commented, "Honestly, if your goal is to limit the damage, you are showing quite a poor performance. Anyway, let us not waste time. I do not need any update from your side. I probably know much more than you do."

Diana said, "Can you tell us where you are now and if you need us to send you a rescue team?"

Wal replied, "I think you will need some rescue from me."

Tommaso could not help smiling: at last somebody able to hold his own against Diana! He was really enjoying the moment, but there were more pressing issues, so he asked, "Ned, where exactly are you now? Did you discover anything more?"

Wal answered, "You bet, Tom. First of all we asked for hospitality in the Greek consulate in Odessa. Up to now they have been very hospitable, but I would not mind if, after this call, you call the Consul up just to be sure he will continue to be that hospitable."

Tommaso questioned back, "You said 'we asked for hospitality'?"

Ned replied plainly, "Yes, we: I and our common friend Shakil, the one sharing the lovely Sheila with Aaron!"

Tommaso was thinking, *OK, the empathy level is exactly the same as Diana's; maybe this is the reason why the go along so well*, but he just asked, "Ned, let's gloss over the details. Aaron is here with us and still quite shocked by the events."

Ned went on, "OK, sorry for the digression. As I was saying, Shakil is here with me. After Sheila's arrest, he flew to Odessa. Don't ask me how I knew it; I have my information channels. I disappeared for a while to be able to act freely. From Kiev I reached Odessa and it was a kid's game to find Shakil. He was trying to get in touch with his connections to understand what to do when the news about Sheila's death arrived here. It did not take long for our friend to realize that he would probably be the next. A dead collaborator is a safe collaborator, above all if he is not indispensable: Shakil was a pawn, a good tech guy useful for the real criminals. He did not know much about the organization beside Sheila and his contact in Odessa. So I could not get much out of him."

Diana interjected, "Please be sure he will not leave the Consulate. We will ask for the extradition soon to be able to interrogate him directly."

Ned replied, "Do as you wish. I do not think Shakil has any desire to go out of here: he would not last half an hour. Nevertheless, I was able to get some useful information out of him. First of all, as I was saying, his role was mainly technical. His task was to go beyond the defenses of TotalHealth and IMD. You know already everything about TotalHealth, right?"

Fred confirmed, "Yes Ned. Social engineering, pure social engineering in the more classical of the possible variants. They were able to get hold of the administrator credentials on the central systems via Rome and to physically break the defenses of one of our outsourcers in East Europe. From our CMDB I believe they were able to retrieve relevant information about our configurations and systems architecture. It's still unclear to me how they managed to overcome IMD defenses: their security levels are much higher than ours."

Ned replied, "Right Fred, right. But as you well know, no system is perfect. And IMD in the last years pushed more on the user friendly interface and "easy-to-maintain" side in its development roadmap. Part of the strategy was the possibility to remotely update all the implanted devices through ISAHBeL and their network of secure wireless connections. But the 'secure' concept is, as you know, never absolute. No system can be 100% secure. You just have to accept a definite risk level."

Martin interjected, "OK, but it would take years even for a good criminal mind to break the security defenses of a company like IMD…"

Ned laughed softly and added, "Martin, don't be naïve. It simply doesn't work that way. It would take years for a single man or for a small group of criminals. But horizontal collaboration, so much preached in so many companies, is a reality among criminals. There are cyber-criminal marketplaces not so different from eBay where access credentials to critical information systems and vulnerabilities can be sold and bought. Criminals work in a network. The 'Internet revolution' did happen for them as well as for us. But while we use the Internet most of the time for video games or to waste time on social networks, they were able to get the most out of the new technologies.

"To be more specific, I'll tell you a story. Imagine that one day a lucky criminal finds a vulnerability in IMD systems. He doesn't fully understand the value of it, but he senses he could make some money out of it. So he posts it on a Russian criminal marketplace, where all the cyber-criminals from east Europe work. Very effective and very difficult to break, since they all communicate in Russian and it's very easy to them to identify a "non-native" Russian speaker. And Russia is not doing much right now to fight them, unless they try to attack Russia itself. So somebody notices the post and proposes a batch of credit card numbers in exchange for it.

"But this new criminal is of a different level. He is not a technician, he is a business man who understands the value of what he has found. With this information in hand, he enters a bigger context, probably out of the small group of Russian cyber-criminals. And here somebody starts putting together a team, with people like Shakil and Sheila, together with many others. Shakil is able enough to use the IMD network vulnerability to enter their systems and to extend the attack to their implanted devices. Now the team is ready for the final attack, as you witnessed ... and we completely lost trace of the first cyber-criminal. I can even advance an hypothesis: IMD and TotalHealth were chosen as targets for the first and third waves of the attack after they found the vulnerability and not before. Something of the like probably happened for communication and energy distribution systems, but maybe the vulnerabilities were not as serious since you were able to stop easily the attack. Maybe on that notorious marketplace there are more IMD vulnerabilities available."

Tommaso could not stop a motion of impatience, "So you are saying there are more vulnerabilities on IMD systems?"

"I believe so", Ned replied, "but probably not directly linked to the devices, so patients should not be in danger any more. If Myriam received the last update she should be safe, at least for now. Other vulnerabilities, at least from what I discovered, are more on IMD network. Shakil gave me some interesting information I transmitted to IMD. I'll forward them to you as well. Anyway, the boy is ready to collaborate and to help IMD and TotalHealth to identify and close the remaining vulnerabilities. I do believe, despite the fact that he will answer to a judge for what he did, his contribution would be fundamental."

Diana said, "That is not for you to decide. Anyway, there are other examples of former cyber-criminals who turned themselves to the right side of the war. We will decide after Shakil's extradition to Canada. For now, I need to ask you to keep yourself and Shakil available in the next hours."

Ned closed the communication with a dry, "As you wish. You will be able to find me at this number at the Greek consulate."

Chapter 31. Jornada del muerto. Location: Canada. Timeline: present time, April 18, 6:30 p.m. local time

Thanks to Wal's information, the last security holes had been closed in IMD systems. Diana asked for a last conference call with Wal to update him. The net result of the last two stormy days was impressive. They were in the meeting room and on CIRANO monitors they could see television news from all over the world. The headlines were always the same: a Canadian city under an unprecedented cyber-attack. The city hospitals were almost useless, 10 people died: 9 patients with IMD pacemakers and one with an implanted IMD insulin pump. Moreover, one patient was injured by abnormal X-rays during an X-ray CT and two technicians were wounded by an unexpected switch-on of a Nuclear Magnetic Resonance. Local authorities ordered the evacuation of the city. The images were repeating in all the transmissions: a long snake of cars, leaving the city under the supervision of civil and military authorities.

Diana started the communication with Wal and when he answered she opened saying, "Thank you for being so kind as to remain available for us. I wanted to update you that emergency extradition procedure for Shakil has been activated. As soon as possible the local police will take him into custody and will transfer him to Canada. I wanted to let you know you are free to move now, since I understand you are well into the night there. You will be brought back to Canada with Shakil tomorrow."

Ned answered, "Very well, it's about time to go back home for me!"

A moment of silence followed: nobody was speaking but a common question was hanging in the air, voiced by Tommaso, "But we did not discuss the real point ... how could all this happen?"

Diana said, "What we expected to happen did happen, but we did not know where and when. After the militarization of the four traditional combat domains, space, sky, sea, and land, the run to militarize the cyberspace has started. This holds true both at the national and military levels and at the criminal organization level. The confrontation is moving more and more to the fifth domain of warfare: cyber-space."

Tommaso said, "So we are at war? But who is the enemy? What will be his next move?"

Diana paused for a while, then answered, "Unfortunately, here is the peculiarity of the Fifth Domain: there are practically no barriers to entry since you do not need big investments to start a war on cyber-space. There are no uniforms or banners. They can hit you in any point of your nervous system: hospitals, transportation, critical infrastructures. And it is extremely hard to discover who is attacking you: it could be a military power, a group of terrorists or a small team of activists. Or it could be a military power hiding behind a group of terrorists or vice versa. And the attack surface of every advanced society is enormous. Translated: is very, very difficult to defend such a perimeter. It's almost like having a bunch of madmen around able to drop a nuclear bomb on a randomly selected city without leaving any useful hint to trace back to the criminal. Anyway, I do not think this was a real war action."

Here it was Ned's time to speak, "What do you mean? So what is it, in your opinion?"

Diana started again, "If this was intended to be a war action, they would probably choose a different target and they would have gone all the way. Why to kill 'only' 9 persons in a Canadian city? IMD patients with attackable implanted devices are all over the world: the IMD CEO told us, before the press-conference, that the security issues were extremely serious and potentially impacted thousands of patients all around the world. The criminals could have easily killed most of them before we could stop them. I think this was a kind of test, a dry run. It's what in ballistics you call, before we started using satellites, indirect fire. They wanted us to assume that was their true target and in the meantime to demonstrate it was possible to cripple a city and force the authorities to evacuate it working only in cyber-space, without firing a single shot or using a bomb. We do not know what their next target will be. We just know that using the global network of two Canadian companies, TotalHealth and IMD, they were able to launch an attack in the very heart of Canada. Maybe the target was chosen because Canada is one of the largest providers of uranium and hydrocarbons for the United States. Or maybe Canada was chosen simply because it had the best conditions for an amplified demonstration effect: high density of TotalHealth Hospitals and IMD patients, right vulnerabilities available in some criminal marketplace."

Ned started again, "Do you have any proof to support your statement that this was not the real target but a kind of 'demonstration'?

Diana answered, "Ned, you see, thanks to your information we were able to decipher some of the key messages, which enabled us to stem the second wave. But we deciphered what seemed like a closing message, I think quite meaningful. The message said simply: 'Jornada del Muerto completed'."

Martin raised an eyebrow and said, "Wow, I would call this a very relevant clue." And noticing Tommaso's questioning look he said, "'Jornada del Muerto' is not simply a Spanish way of reminding us of the many deaths of these days. You should know, Tommaso, about the Manhattan project: one of your greatest scientists was part of it, Enrico Fermi. Jornada del Muerto is place in the desert of New Mexico where the scientists performed the last nuclear test before Hiroshima and Nagasaki."

After a long silence, Ned spoke first, "You know I am not an optimistic guy, but I think in a way, this is an opportunity as well: we had the chance to make evident to everybody our weaknesses and vulnerabilities. Now everyone sees what we well knew: cyber-space is no longer a virtual world. A cyber-attack can kill real people in the real world. Ungoverned technology is a mortal threat. But the same technology, wisely governed, has an incredible potential to improve our lives. It allows us to be more efficient, freeing us from mechanical and repetitive operations. We can cure our patients remotely, in some cases even performing surgery remotely. We can communicate easily and better than in the past. Maybe it's about time to manage technology, not only in terms of efficiency and effectiveness, but using common sense as well. We do not really know what's in front of us: this could be the announcement of a new and more dangerous attack or simply a show of brute force for the benefit of potential clients of a new mercenary cyber-army. Whatever is the meaning of all of this, what we should get out of it is that technology is a dangerous toy and we can no longer handle it with foolishness: as we prepared ourselves to defend the physical borders of our world, from now on we should be ready to defend ourselves even in the Fifth Domain."

APPENDIX TO PART III: FAQS & FACTS

Q) Is really possible to hack an implanted medical device?
A) I really would like to answer no. But unfortunately you will find more than one article in the web about it. I'd start by quoting a paragraph from a HIMSS article:

> "Two years ago, security expert Jerome Radcliffe made news for hacking his own insulin pump with less than $20 worth of technology. Then, at a security conference last fall, late IOActive researcher Barnaby Jack claimed that he could hack a pacemaker from 50 feet away, causing it to deliver a lethal 830-volt shock. He likened his hack to an "anonymous assassination." Even former Vice President Dick Cheney recently revealed that he had his pacemaker's wireless utility disabled as a pre-emptive security measure."

Here is the link to the full article:
http://www.himssfuturecare.com/blog/hacking-your-heart
I could add a few more links:
http://rt.com/usa/us-warns-medical-cyberattack-721/
http://www.economist.com/blogs/economist-explains/2013/06/economist-explains-5
http://www.forbes.com/sites/singularity/2012/12/06/yes-you-can-hack-a-pacemaker-and-other-medical-devices-too/
Alternatively try to google: "hacking implanted medical devices".

Q) Why are CIOs so concerned about systems traditionally out of their responsibility?
A) Basically for two reasons. The first and the most important is that quite often, as in the case of diagnostic equipment and implantable medical devices, these systems have an extremely high level of risk, sometimes threatening the lives of the patients. Until a few years ago, they were basically "closed systems" with very limited IT components, so traditionally they were out of scope for CIOs. However, in the past 10 years, the complexity of the IT components has increased

constantly. Nowadays almost every diagnostic equipment combines the traditional equipment with a client/server application to manage data and to automate processes. The same holds true for implantable devices.

The second reason is that raising the security protection on traditional IT systems and not doing it on medical devices/equipment, for example, is an illusion, since usually those systems share common resources (the network), have the same users and data are exchanged (manually or through integrations) among them. Unfortunately the problem is not limited to healthcare. Read this article from ISA, the International Society of Automation:
http://www.isa.org/InTechTemplate.cfm?Section=Communities&template=/TaggedPage/DetailDisplay.cfm&ContentID=69056
Or:
http://www.accenture.com/SiteCollectionDocuments/PDF/Accenture-MES-Who-Owns-Information-Systems-plant.pdf.
Alternatively google: "accenture who owns mes systems"

I will cite two sentences: (Accenture Report) — *"In the ISA-95 standard classification of industrial applications, MES (Manufacturing Execution Systems) is part of the level 3 technology, or industrial IT. This level is not yet clearly defined at most large companies; as a result, there is typically no formal definition of who should oversee these applications. The information technology (IT) group and operations/automation technology (AT) group are both involved in overseeing level 3 applications. But experience has shown that often, neither of these groups has the full range of skills and knowledge needed to provide effective MES governance."*

(ISA article) — *"IT departments traditionally handle ERP and other systems used in the office. The functionality in these systems, like order processing, administrative material management, and cost accounting, belongs largely to ISA95*

level 4. These IT people 'speak' Java, .Net, and other programming languages. Engineers are working in a completely different world, namely the world of instrumentation, PLC, SCADA, and DCS with programming languages like ladder diagram, SFC, and function blocks. They are active on ISA95 levels 2, 1 and 0. But who takes care of the automation of activities at ISA95 level 3, often called the MES layer? This is about activities like finite production scheduling, recipe management, data collection, tracking, and tracing. Traditional level 2 process control system vendors have offered more level 3 functionality over time, with historians, standard production reporting, and recipe management. These systems closely integrate with the systems on level 2, so it is essential to have thorough knowledge of the process and its automation. This suggests engineers are the ones to support MES and execute MES projects. On the other hand, there are reasons to think MES should be supported by IT. MES software vendors have based their historians, reporting functionality and recipe management on the operating systems, programming languages and network protocols characteristic for IT environments. Moreover, the term Manufacturing IT is becoming more predominant today."

Q) What is a CERT or CSIRT?
A) From the European Union Agency for Network and Information Security (ENISA) *http://www.enisa.europa.eu/activities/cert/support/guide2/introduction/what-is-csirt* :
"CSIRT stands for Computer Security Incident Response Team. The name CSIRT is the name used predominantly in Europe for the protected CERT® or CERT-CC name.
The following abbreviations are used for the same sort of teams:
- CERT® or CERT-CC (Computer Emergency Response Team / Coordination Center)
- CSIRT (Computer Security Incident Response Team)

- IRT (Incident Response Team)
- CIRT (Computer Incident Response Team)
- SERT (Security Emergency Response Team)

The first major outbreak of a worm in the global ICT infrastructure occurred in the late 1980s. This worm was named after his creator, Morris, and spread swiftly, effectively infecting a great number of ICT systems around the world."

This incident acted as a wake-up call: suddenly people became aware of a strong need for cooperation and coordination between system administrators and IT managers in order to deal with cases like this. Due to the fact that time was a critical factor, a more organized and structured approach for handling IT security incidents had to be established. And so a few days after the "Morris-incident" the Defense Advanced Research Projects Agency (DARPA) established the first CSIRT: the CERT Coordination Center (CERT/CC), located at the Carnegie Mellon University in Pittsburgh (Pennsylvania). This model was soon adopted within Europe, and 1992 the Dutch Academic provider SURFnet launched the first CSIRT in Europe, named SURFnet-CERT. Many teams followed and at present ENISAs Inventory of CERT activities in Europe (ENISA Inventory) lists more than 100 known teams located in Europe.

Over the years CERTs extended their capacities from being a mere reaction force to a complete security service provider, including preventative services such as alerts, security advisories, training and security management services. The term "CERT" was soon considered insufficient. As a result, the new term "CSIRT" was established at the end of the1990s. At the moment both terms (CERT and CSIRT) are used synonymously, with CSIRT being the more precise term.

[...] A CSIRT is a team that responds to computer security incidents by providing all necessary services to solve the problem(s) or to support their resolution.

PS: in the novel the role of the Canadian CIRANO team is much "broader" than the definition reported implies: it is a sort of evolution of the CSIRT concept, mixing security and police powers. The CIRANO team depicted in the novel, with Diana and her staff, is non-existent in reality.

Q) Does something like a "cyber-criminal marketplace" exist in reality?
A) Again, I would like to answer no. But indeed there is more than one marketplace of this kind. The most famous was probably DarkMarket. Here there are a couple of interesting links: *http://en.wikipedia.org/wiki/DarkMarket*
http://www.theguardian.com/technology/2010/jan/14/darkmarket-online-fraud-trial-wembley – alternatively google: "dark market cyber crime".

If you want to know more, there is an interesting book by Misha Glenny, "DarkMarket: How Hackers Became the New Mafia." In the book Glenny starts from the famous criminal forum and tracks down the key players of the underground crime network.

Q) Where does the expression "Fifth Domain" come from?
A) The term "Fifth Domain" was first used in an article published in The Economist *(http://www.economist.com/node/16481504?story_id=16481504&source=features_box1).*

The article says, "Cyberspace has become the fifth domain of warfare, after land, sea, air and space." But more interesting are other passages in the same article. The article is quite old nowadays but many topics are still relevant, so I'd like to close the novel part of this book quoting them, "THROUGHOUT history new technologies have revolutionized warfare, sometimes abruptly, sometimes only gradually: think of the chariot, gunpowder, aircraft, radar and nuclear fission. So it has been with information technology. Computers and the Internet have transformed economies and given Western armies great advantages, such as the ability to send remotely piloted aircraft across the world to gather intelligence and attack targets. But the spread of digital technology comes at a cost: it exposes armies and societies to digital attack. The threat is complex, multifaceted and potentially very dangerous. Modern societies are ever more reliant on computer systems linked to the Internet, giving enemies more avenues of attack. If power stations, refineries, banks and air-traffic control systems were brought down, people would lose their lives. Yet there are few, if any, rules in cyberspace of the kind that govern behavior, even warfare, in other domains. [...]

The cyber-attacks on Estonia in 2007 and on Georgia in 2008 (the latter strangely happened to coincide with the advance of Russian troops across the Caucasus) are widely assumed to have been directed by the Kremlin, but they could be traced only to Russian cyber-criminals. Many of the computers used in the attack belonged to innocent Americans whose PCs had been hijacked. [...] Cyber-weapons are being developed secretly, without discussion of how and when they might be used. Nobody knows their true power, so countries must prepare for the worst. Anonymity adds to the risk that mistakes, misattribution and miscalculation will lead to military escalation—with conventional weapons or cyber arms. [...]

One response to this growing threat has been military. Iran claims to have the world's second-largest cyber-army. Russia, Israel and North Korea boast efforts of their own. America has set up its new Cyber Command both to defend its networks and devise attacks on its enemies. NATO is debating the extent to which it should count cyberwar as a form of "armed attack" that would oblige its members to come to the aid of an ally.

[...] If cyber arms-control is to America's advantage, it would be wise to shape such accords while it still has the upper hand in cyberspace. General Keith Alexander, the four-star general who heads Cyber Command, is therefore right to welcome Russia's longstanding calls for a treaty as a *"starting point for international debate." That said, a START-style treaty may prove impossible to negotiate. Nuclear warheads can be counted and missiles tracked. Cyber-weapons are more like biological agents; they can be made just about anywhere."*

Well, I think there is enough material for another book ...

If you want to know more about how the reality can go beyond fiction, read the appendices to chapters 17 to 31 at the end of the book, collecting selected posts from John D. Halamka's blog, LIFE AS A HEALTHCARE CIO.

APPENDICES FROM "LIFE AS A HEALTHARE CIO"

Appendix to Chapter 1: How the breakdown of a critical IT system (network) impacted on CareGroup hospitals activities.

LIFE AS A HEALTHCARE CIO: The CareGroup Network Outage (March 4 2008 post)

On November 13, 2002 at 1:45pm, Beth Israel Deaconess Medical Center went from the hospital of 2002 to the hospital of 1972. Network traffic stopped. No clinician could order medications or labs electronically. No decision support was available. Luckily, no patients were harmed. Here's the story of what happened and our lessons learned.

In the years after the 1996 merger of the Beth Israel and Deaconess Hospitals, operating losses caused several years of capital starvation (the network budget in 2002 was $50,000 for the entire $2 billion dollar enterprise). We were not available to invest in infrastructure, so our network components were beyond their useful life.

However, it was not this infrastructure underinvestment that was the root cause of the problem, it was my lack of enterprise network infrastructure knowledge. I did not know what I did not know. Here are the details:

1. Our Network topology was perfectly architected for 1996. Back in the days when the internet was a friendly place where all internal and external collaborators could be trusted, a switched core (layer 2) that transmitted all packets from place to place was a reasonable design. After 1996, the likelihood of denial of service attacks, trojans, or other malware meant that networks should be routed and highly segmented, isolating any bad actors to a constrained local area. At the time of our outage, a data flood in one part of the network propagated to every other part of the network - a bit like living downstream from a dam that collapsed. A well meaning researcher created a napster-like application that began exchanging hundreds of gigabytes of data via multicast to multiple collaborators. The entire network was so saturated that we could not diagnose the root cause of the data flood. I did not know that a switched core was a point of failure.

2. Our Network team was managed by a very smart engineer who did not share all his knowledge with the network team. Much of our network configuration was poorly documented. With the knowledge of our network isolated to one person, we had a single point of human failure. I did not know that this engineer was unfamiliar with the best practices for routed/redundant network cores, routed distribution layers and switched access layers isolated into vlans with quality of service configurations to prevent monopolization of bandwidth by any one user or application. We brought in a Cisco partner, Callisma, to document the network, but the network failure occurred before they were finished.

3. I did not know about spanning tree algorithms, hot standby routing protocols (HSRP), and Open Shortest Path First (OSPF). During the outage, I approved configuration changes that actually made the situation worse by causing spanning tree propagations, flooding the network with even more traffic.

4. I did not establish a relationship with the vendor (Cisco) that enabled them to warn me about our vulnerabilities. A relationship with a vendor can take many forms, ranging from a sales driven vendor/client adversarial relationship to a collaborative partnership. In 2002, Cisco was just another vendor we purchased from. Today they are a collaborative partner with a seat at the table when we plan new infrastructure.

5. I did not know that we needed "out of band" tools to gain insight into the problems with the network. In effect, we required the network to be functional to diagnose problems with the network.

6. We did not have a robust, tested downtime plan for a total network collapse. When the outage occurred, we rapidly designed new processes to transport lab results, orders, and other data via runners from place to place.

7. We did not have a robust communication plan for responding to a total network collapse. Email, web-based paging, portals, and anything that used the data network for communication was down. Voice mail broadcasts using our PBX and regular phones (not IP phones) turned out to save the day.

8. When we diagnosed the problem, we explored many root causes and made many changes in the hope that we'd find the magic bullet to cure the problem. In the end, we ended up fixing many basic structural problems in the network, which took 2 days and eventually solved the problem. A more expedient solution would have been to reverse all changes we made in our attempts to fix the network once we had stopped the internal attack. When a crisis occurs, making changes on top of changes can make diagnosis and remediation even more difficult.

9. We did not have an enterprise wide change control process to ensure that every network configuration, server addition, and software enhancement was documented and assessed for impact on security, stability, and performance. Today we have a weekly change control board that include includes all IS departments, Cisco engineering services, and IS leadership to assess and communicate all configuration changes.

10. I was risk averse and did not want to replace the leadership of the network team for fear that terminating our single point of human failure would result in an outage. The price of keeping the leadership in place was a worse outage. I should have acted sooner to bolster leadership of the team.

Despite the pain and stress of the outage, there was a "lemons to lemonade" ending. Without this incident, the medical center *would never have realized the importance of investing in basic IT infrastructure. If not for the "perfect storm", we may have limped along with a marginal network for years.*

Today, we receive annual capital funding to support a regular refresh of our technology base, and we are asked to introduce change at a pace that is manageable. People in the medical center still remember the outage and are more accepting of a tightly managed infrastructure such as locked down workstations, security precautions, disaster recovery initiatives, and maintenance downtime windows.

[...] I hope that my experience will help other organizations prevent network and other IT outages in the future.

Detailed description of the event is included in F. Warren McFarlan - Robert D. Austin Case Study "CareGroup" for Harvard Business School

Appendix to Chapter 2: The Zombie computers

LIFE AS A HEALTHCARE CIO: The Growing Malware Problem (November 9 2011 post)

Have you ever seen a Zombie film? If so, you know that to stop Zombies you must shoot them in the head - the only problem is that the steady stream of Zombies never seems to end and they keep infecting others. Just when you've eradicated every Zombie but one, the infection gets transmitted and the problem returns. You spend your day shooting them but you never seem to make any progress.

A Zombie in computer science is a computer connected to the Internet that has been compromised by a cracker, computer virus or trojan horse and can be used to perform malicious tasks of one sort or another under remote direction.

Starting in March of 2011, the rise in malware on the internet has created millions of zombie computers. Experts estimate that 48% of all computers on the internet are infected. Malware is transmitted from infected photos (Heidi Klum is the most dangerous celebrity on the internet this year), infected PDFs, infected Java files, ActiveX controls that take advantage of Windows/Internet Explorer vulnerabilities and numerous other means.

Here's the problem - the nature of this new malware is that it is hard to detect (often hiding on hard disk boot tracks), it's hard to remove (often requiring complete reinstallation of the operating system), and anti-virus software no longer works against it.

A new virus is released on the internet every 30 seconds. Modern viruses contain self modifying code. The "signature" approaches used in anti-virus software to rapidly identify known viruses, does not work with this new generation of malware.

Android attacks have increased 400% in the past year. Even the

Apple.

Apple OS X is not immune. Experts estimate that some recent viruses infections are 15% Mac.

If attacks are escalating and our existing tools to prevent them do not work, what must we do?

Alas, we must limit inbound and outbound traffic to corporate networks.

BIDMC will pilot increased restrictions in a few departments to determine if it reduces the amount of malware we detect and eradicate. I'll report on the details over the next few months.

One of these restrictions will be increased web content filtering. I predict in a few years, that corporate networks will advance from content filtering to more restrictive "white listing". Instead of blocking selective content categories, they will allow only those websites reputed to be safe (at that moment anyway). I think it is likely corporate networks will block personal email, auction sites, and those social networking sites which are vectors for malware.

It's truly tragic that the internet has become such a swamp, especially at a time that we want to encourage the purchase of consumer devices such as tablets and smartphones.

I've said before that security is a cold war. Unfortunately, starting in March, the malware authors launched an assault on us all. We'll need to take urgent action to defend ourselves and I'll update you on our pilots to share our successful tactics.

Appendix to Chapter 5: The marriage between business and IT

LIFE AS A HEALTHCARE CIO: Defining Business Requirements (December 29 2010 post)

In my roles at various institutions, I've had the opportunity to work with thousands of highly diverse stakeholders. Some are IT savvy, some are not. Some are project management savvy, some are not. Some understand leading practices for their particular departmental functions, some do not.

Here's what I've learned.

1. Automating a dysfunctional manual process will not yield a successful performance improvement outcome. Before any technology project is launched, the business owners need to understand their own process flows and goals for improving them.

2. If business owners cannot define their future state workflows, software is not going to do it for them. Sometimes, business owners tell me "I need to buy a wonderful niche software package from XYZ vendor." When I ask how they will use it, they answer that the software will define their workflow for them.

3. The IT department can impose governance and project management processes to ensure that future state workflows and requirements are defined prior to any procurement processes. However, the business owners who are least experienced with project management methodology will accuse the IT department of slowing down the purchase. One way around this is to create an institutional project management office outside of the IT department which serves as a bridge between the business owners and the IT organization providing the service. Such an approach adds expert resources to the department requesting automation to lead them through a requirements definition process as a first step. Projects without clear requirements and goals can be stopped before they expend time and money on an implementation that is likely to fail.

4. Some departments will try to circumvent governance prioritization and project management processes by contributing departmental funds, obtaining a grant, or getting a donor to fund their software purchases. Such as approach should not be allowed for many reasons. Software licensing is generally about 20% of total implementation cost which includes hardware, configuration, interfacing, testing, training, and support costs. Every software implementation is a project and needs to be considered a use of scarce IT resources. It is reasonable to initiate an automation request through a project management office to define business requirements and goals, then present it to a governance process for prioritization, then fund the total project costs via departmental/grant/donor dollars if the project is deemed a high priority for implementation.

5. Creating formal documentation of business requirements, goals/success metrics, and forecasted financial impact is important to establish ownership of the project by the sponsoring department. Although infrastructure projects such as provisioning networks, desktops, storage, and servers can be owned by the IT department, application projects should never be owned or sponsored by the IT department. The business owner, working with the institutional project management office, needs to drive the implementation to achieve the desired process improvement and to ensure appropriate change management. If the project is considered an IT effort, then business owners will claim their lack of requirements definition or process redesign is an IT failure based on poorly designed or implemented software.

Thus, however unpopular it makes the CIO, insist on business owner sponsorship with defined requirements, goals, and accountability for process and people change management.

Every project I've been involved in that includes this role for the business owner has been successful. With clearly defined responsibilities and accountability, customer satisfaction with these projects has been high, because business owners feel compelled to make the project a success rather than expect IT to deliver a finished project to them.

Appendix to Chapter 6: Personal Health Records and two particular situations

HBR Blog Network: Be the CEO of Your Medical Information (March 30 2009, J. D. Halamka post)

You probably take for granted that you should manage your own resume and C.V. They catalog your professional history and accomplishments — who else would manage them well? But chances are you don't oversee your own medical records. Until now, that's been difficult to do, because bits and pieces of your medical information are probably scattered across the records of several doctors, hospitals, labs, and pharmacies. It's an inconvenient — and potentially dangerous — state of affairs, but one that a new federal law may help to remedy.

The American Recovery and Reinvestment Act provides $34 billion for improving the exchange of health care information. One trickle-down effect will likely be greater access to your lifetime medical information through a personal health record that is in electronic form. The underlying idea is simple: Compiling your medical data in one place lets you be the steward of your health information.

Although creating a personal health record initially takes time, just as drafting a first C.V. does, there are several payoffs. Having the record can prevent unnecessary testing and treatment, reduce the chance of a medication error, and instantly provide vital information in an emergency. It also can be a dynamic health tracker of body weight, blood sugar, and much more. In short, a personal health record can reduce costs and improve the quality of the care you receive. At a minimum, it should contain:

- *your name, date of birth, and vital statistics such as height and weight*
- *a list of emergency contacts, along with contact information for all your health care providers*
- *information about your health insurance*
- *a brief history of your health, as well as a list of illnesses and conditions your parents, grandparents, and siblings have had*
- *a dated list of significant illnesses and hospitalizations*
- *your current health conditions and how they are being treated*
- *information about allergies or sensitivities to medications*
- *an inventory of the medications you take, including dosages and frequency*
- *lab test results*
- *a dated list of immunizations*
- *copies of your living will and durable power of attorney for health care, if you have them.*

So far, four types of electronic personal health record products are available:

Hospital- and clinician-hosted records are great if all your information resides at one institution. An example of this type of system is PatientSite, used by more than 40,000 patients of Beth Israel Deaconess Medical Center to view their hospital records, send secure e-mail to doctors, make appointments, refill prescriptions online, and so on. However, a new study in the New England Journal of Medicine highlights an important caveat: Only about 9% of U.S. acute-care hospitals surveyed have an electronic-records system in place in at least one clinical unit.

Payer-hosted records, such as HPHConnect from Harvard Pilgrim Health Care, offer access to your claims information, help you review the resources you are using, and sometimes let you share information with family members or doctors. Drawbacks include a lack of details about lab and radiology results, and no guarantee that you can take the record with you if you change insurers.

Employer-sponsored records are typically hosted by a trusted outside firm, creating a firewall between the employer and the medical data. For example, computer storage giant EMC partnered with WebMD to offer claims-based personal health records to all of its employees. Employer-sponsored systems generally focus on keeping you healthy and productive. They can also help you manage your health care spending account. However, you may not be able to take an employer-hosted record with you if you change jobs.

Commercial offerings such as Google Health and Microsoft HealthVault empower you to link to your electronic records at participating hospitals, pharmacies, and laboratories. You can pull in your existing data and add your own; search for information about drug interactions and your medical conditions; and share it all with appropriate stakeholders, including your doctors. These products enable you to keep your health record for life, regardless of your job or insurer. Google recently implemented secure "social networking" for personal health records. Call it Facebook for health care. It allows you to invite caregivers or family members to access your personal health information. Invitees can be removed at any time.

What about privacy? Each of these products has strict policies not to mine personal health data, share them, or use them for targeted advertising. Hospital and payer data are covered by rules in the Health Insurance Portability and Accountability Act of 1996 (HIPAA). The Google and Microsoft offerings are outside HIPAA's scope, but both companies have developed policies that are even stronger than HIPAA's. I trust the policies enough to have stored my lifetime medical record on Google Health and Microsoft HealthVault. (I share it with you here at my own discretion.) Whatever record system you choose, make sure it has strict privacy policies that keep you in control of the information at all times.

This new world of connected health care, with you in charge of your medical information, has tremendous potential in terms of both personal and system-wide efficiency. What's in your interest complements what's in the interest of the larger health care system as we try to reduce costs and improve care.

Have you created a personal health record yet? Do you think you might?

LIFE AS A HEALTHCARE CIO: Personal Health Records Use by Adolescents (May 15 2013 post)

In response to many questions about PHR use by adolescents, I asked Fabienne Bourgeois, the expert at Children's Hospital Boston, to write this guest blog post -

As more and more practices and hospitals are making patient portals available to their patients, providers of adolescent patients are encountering a major hurdle: how to handle confidential adolescent information.

While adult patients generally maintain full personal control of their personal health record (PHR), adolescent PHRs are anything but personal. Adolescents rarely have full control of their record, but instead rely on parents and guardians to share control. The details around this shared access changes over time, depending on developmental and age-appropriate considerations, as well as guardianship arrangements.

The biggest challenge then, becomes how to protect the adolescent's legal right to privacy and confidentiality within this hybrid/proxy-control model. Many medical encounters with adolescents come with the verbal assurance that what they tell us will (under most circumstances) remain entirely confidential, meaning we will not discuss personal health information pertaining to reproductive health, sexually transmitted diseases, substance abuse and mental health with their parents or anyone else without their consent. As it turns out, this type of confidential information is pervasive through most EHRs.

We've spent a lot of time thinking about this issue and adolescent access to our patient portal, and ultimately developed a custom built solution to meet our and our patients' needs.

Our approach is built around differential access to the patient portal with the goal of mirroring current clinical practice and works as follows:

Access to the patient portal: Separate accounts are created for the patient and parent(s) that are linked. The parent has sole access to the patient's portal until the patient turns 13, at which point both the parent and the patient can have access. We chose 13 years as our cut off based on a number of factors, including developmental maturity and other precedents at our institution based on their policies. At 18 years, the patient becomes the sole owner of the portal account, and we deactivate the parent's link (unless we receive court documents stating that the parent remains the medical guardian).

Health information contained in the patient portal: We have identified and tagged certain information from our EHR that we consider sensitive, such as labs related to pregnancy, sexually transmitted illnesses, genetic results, select confidential appointments, and potentially sensitive problems and medications. This information is currently filtered from both parent and adolescent accounts, but in the near future the sensitive information will flow to the adolescent account, but not to the parent account. So, even if a patient is less than 13 years, the parent would not have access to this information.
This solution does take a lot of time and effort, but best replicates the current clinical practice. Many other current PHR structures do not allow for this type of differential access and only enable full proxy access.

Alternative solutions include the following:
1. Shared access for patient and parent, but filtering of sensitive information. One could then choose the age at which patients would gain access without worrying about the parent seeing sensitive information at any age. This makes the age at which the patient obtains access, whether it is 10 or 13 years, less important. Unfortunately, this option restricts adolescent access to confidential information and creates a fragmented and incomplete record.

2. *Adolescent access only. This is trickier, because choosing the appropriate age when parental access is discontinued is difficult and may vary depending on patient characteristics. Many practices choose 12 or 13 years. However, if sensitive information is not being filtered, you may very well have the occasional 11 year old with an STI. Also, some parents object to being cut off from their child's medical information and many play an important role in supporting their adolescent children and guiding them through healthcare decisions.*

The issues and solutions involved with adolescent PHRs are certainly complex and will continue to evolve over time. However, I am hopeful that PHRs will start incorporating the unique needs of the adolescent population in the near future, allowing both parents and adolescents to share responsibility and engage in their healthcare.

For additional information, see this publication

Bourgeois FC, Taylor PL, Emans SJ, Nigrin DJ, Mandl KD. Whose personal control? Creating Private, Personally Controlled Health Records for Pediatric and Adolescent Patients J. Am. Med. Inform. Assoc. 2008;15(6):737-743

LIFE AS A HEALTHCARE CIO: A Chip in My Shoulder (December 18 2007 post)

I'm often asked about the RFID chip containing my medical records which is implanted in my right arm.

As a physician and chief information officer, I felt qualified to evaluate the medical, legal, moral, and privacy aspects of the device. After using the device for three years, I am not an evangelist for implanted RFID, but I believe it can be valuable for some patients who understand the risks and benefits. My implantation process in December 2004 was simple—a five minute office procedure, which included disinfection of the implant site on my upper right arm, a few cubic centimeters of lidocaine, and insertion of the injector into my subcutaneous fascia. I did not experience pain, bleeding, or any post-procedure infection. The implant is not palpable, does not migrate, and has no physical side effects such as itching, irritation, or changes in skin appearance. The RFID device does not impede my activities; even while rock or ice climbing I have hit the implant site many times without any problems. The device is undetectable by airport security metal detectors and hand scanners.

One possible side effect is that my RFID device can be scanned by retail security systems using 134.2 kHz RFID technology, the frequency of my implant. I have had experiences at Home Depot and Best Buy where my device seemed to set off the anti-theft systems. My personal data are not readable by such systems, but they may be able to detect the presence of an implanted RFID tag.

Given my experience, what are the risks and benefits? The medical risks of any implant are infection, pain, keloid formation at the puncture site, and reaction to the local anesthetic. There are quite a range of nonmedical risks. After my implant, I received many e-mails saying that I had become a "Borg" and had lost some of my humanity because I was now a hybrid human/machine. Some e-mails even referred to the Book of

Revelation, noting that I now carried the number of the Beast. Thus, chip carriers have a risk of being social outcasts.

The chip holds a static and unencrypted 16 digit number, which is used to point to a Web site containing personal health record data. The Web site requires a username and password, ensuring appropriate security. It is conceivable that a person on a subway could scan a patient's number without their knowledge and steal their medical identity by creating an identical chip and implanting it. This is a very theoretical risk because hospitals are not widely using implanted RFID chips as a means of identification. If the implanted chip were used for security purposes, such as opening a door to a secure area, the person who scanned the patient on the subway could replay the RFID signal and gain access to the secure area. Again, this is purely theoretical since implanted RFID devices are not often used as security authenticators.

If these are the potential risks, what are the benefits? Since we have no universal health identifier in the US, there is no simple way to uniquely identify a patient at all sites of care. The result is a fractured medical record scattered in inpatient, outpatient, laboratory, pharmacy, and emergency department sites. The implanted RFID devices enable patients to establish health care identities and become the stewards of their own data. The patient can assemble a reconciled medication list, a complete problem list, and a list of diagnostic study results, and then apply personal privacy preferences—for example, deleting information about mental health, HIV, or substance abuse. This patient-controlled record is available to treating clinicians in the case of emergency via the implanted device.

It is a personal choice whether or not to be fitted with an RFID device, but for some patients such a record has value. For example, such devices may be particularly helpful for a patient with Alzheimer disease who cannot give a history, a patient prone to syncope who may not be initially conscious during an emergency department visit, or a very active person who engages in extreme sports activities and could be noncommunicative due to injury.

I believe that in the near future, patients will own their medical records and be the stewards of their own health care data. Implantation of RFID devices is one tool, appropriate for some patients based on their personal analysis of risks and benefits, that can empower patients by serving as a source of identity and a link to a personal health record when the patient cannot otherwise communicate.

Appendix to Chapter 7: Identity is the key point!

LIFE AS A HEALTHCARE CIO: Strong Identity Management (December 2 2009 post)

In addition to audit trails, a key component of enforcing security policy is ensuring the identity of those who use applications. In the November 19th HIT Standards Committee testimony, we heard about the need for strong identity management.

Currently, most systems support username/password with various rules such as those we use as BIDMC:

*Passwords must be at least eight (8) characters in length
Passwords must contain characters from at least three (3) of the following four (4) classes:
English upper case letters A,B,C,...Z
English lower case letters a,b,c,...z
Westernized Arabic numerals 0,1,2,...9
Non-alphanumeric ("special characters") such as punctuation symbols: !,@,#...
New passwords must be different from previously used passwords.
Under no circumstances should the Passwords contain your username or any part of your full name or other easily identifiable information.*

However, it's clear that something stronger than a username/password will be needed for e-prescribing controlled substances. The DEA has insisted upon NIST Level 3 authentication. What do levels of authentication mean?

Level 1 is the lowest assurance and Level 4 is the highest. The levels are based on the degree of confidence needed in the process used to establish identity and in the proper use of the established credentials.

Level 1 - Little or no confidence in the asserted identity's validity. Level 1 requires little or no confidence in the asserted identity. No identity proofing is required at this level, but the authentication mechanism should provide some assurance that the same claimant is accessing the protected transaction or data.

Level 2 - Some confidence in the asserted identity's validity. Level 2 requires confidence that the asserted identity is accurate. Level 2 provides for single-factor remote network authentication, including identity-proofing requirements for presentation of identifying materials or information.

Level 3 - High confidence in the asserted identity's validity. Level 3 is appropriate for transactions that need high confidence in the accuracy of the asserted identity. Level 3 provides multifactor remote network authentication.

Level 4 - Very high confidence in the asserted identity's valid. Level 4 is for transactions that need very high confidence in the accuracy of the asserted identity. Level 4 provides the highest practical assurance of remote network authentication. Authentication is based on proof of possession of a key through a cryptographic protocol.

If Level 3 authentication is implemented in healthcare for prescribing controlled substances, strong identity management may be expanded to other aspects of healthcare such as signing notes, signing orders, or gaining physical access to restricted areas.

Given the workflow implications of an added authentication burden, it's important to choose the right technology approach.

There are a wide range of two-factor authentication methods, including security tokens, smart cards, biometrics, certificates, soft tokens, and cell phone-based approaches.

I've had experience with each of these. Here's a summary of my findings

Tokens - you'd think tokens would be easy to use, but we had a high login failure rate, challenges with tokens getting lost/destroyed (in the laundry), time synchronization issues (as the battery begins to age, the clock inside the token may begin running slowly), and clinician dissatisfaction with having to carry yet another device. A clinician with multiple affiliations has an even worse problem - multiple tokens to carry around. Token and licensing costs were expensive.

Smart cards - we use smart cards for physical access and they work well. They are foolproof to use, can be laundered without an issue, and are inexpensive. The only problem with using them in software authentication is the expense of adding smart card readers to our 8000 workstations. Buying and maintaining 8000 USB devices is costly. However, they are still a serious consideration, since clinicians like the idea of walking up to a device and using something they already have - a badge - to authenticate.

Biometrics - I've written about our use of BIO-key in the Emergency Department. Biometrics are convenient because you can just swipe a finger, which you always have with you (we hope). Many laptops have built in finger print readers and the BIO-key software easily integrates web applications into Active Directory. As with smart cards, the only challenge is installing and maintaining fingerprint scanners on 8000 existing desktops. Biometrics have been very popular with our clinicians and we've had a very low false negative rate (and zero false positives).

Certificates - managing certificates for 20,000 users is painful. We've done it and although I am a strong believer in organization level certificates, I remain unconvinced that user level certificates are a good idea. Maybe new approaches like Microsoft's Infocard, which presents digitally signed XML-based credentials, *will make storage and presentation of cryptographic credentials easier.*

Soft tokens are just a software version of hardware token running on a mobile device or desktop. Since software must be installed and maintained on each device, they can be a challenge to support.

Cell phone based approaches - Harvard Medical School recently implemented two factor authentication with cell phones as a way of securing password reset functions. It's been popular, easy to support, and very low cost. Companies such as Anakam offer tools and technology to implement strong identify management in cell phones via text messaging, voice delivery of a PIN, or voice biometric verification. Per the Anakam website, their products achieve full compliance with NIST Level 3, are scalable to millions of users, cost less than hard tokens or smart codes, are installable in the enterprise without added client hardware/software, and are easy to use (all you have to do is answer a phone call or read a text message).

Thus, my vote for achieving NIST Level 3 is to choose among smart cards, biometrics or cell phone based approaches depending on the problem to be solved and the workflow that is being automated. Although we've not yet implemented cell phone approaches for EHR authentication, I can imagine that our 2011 authentication strategy might be:

Physical Access (hundreds of existing doors that have smart card readers) - Smart cards

Fast trusted login in the Emergency Department (100 devices that are kept in a closed physical space) - Biometrics

Generalized two factor authentication for e-prescribing controlled substances (thousands of devices and hundreds of users) - Cell phone approaches

With strong identity management, our audit trails will have greater value. It will be challenging for a user to claim that they were not the person performing the transaction. The combination of trusted identity and complete audit trails is key to a multi-layered defense against privacy breeches.

Appendix to Chapter 10: The cloud needs a concrete strategy

LIFE AS A HEALTHCARE CIO: What is our cloud strategy? (December 5 2010 post)

Recently I was asked to define our cloud strategy.
My answer to this is simple. The public cloud (defined as the rapid provisioning and de-provisioning of CPU cycles, software licenses, and storage) is good for many things, such as web hosting or non-critical applications that do not contain patient or confidential information. At Harvard Medical School and Beth Israel Deaconess Medical Center, we've embraced public cloud technology, but transformed it into something with a guaranteed service level and compliance with Federal/State security regulations - the private cloud.

Here's the approach we're using to create private clouds at HMS and BIDMC:

1. At HMS, we created Orchestra, a 6000 core blade-based supercomputer backed by a petabyte of distributed storage. Thousands of users run millions of jobs. It's housed in Harvard controlled space, protected by a multi-layered security strategy, and engineered to be highly available. We also use grid computing technologies to share CPU among multiple high performance computing facilities nationwide.

2. At BIDMC and its physician organization (BIDPO), we've created a virtualized environment for 150 clinician offices, hosting 20 instances of logically isolated electronic health record applications per physical CPU. It's backed with half a petabyte of storage in a fault tolerant networking configuration and is housed at a commercial high availability co-location center.

3. At BIDMC, our clinical systems are run on geographically separated clusters built with high availability blade-based Linux

machines backed by thin-provisioned storage pools.

Each of our private clouds has very high bandwidth internet connections with significant throughput (terabytes per day at HMS). The bandwidth charges of public clouds would be cost prohibitive.

We are investigating the use of public cloud providers to host websites with low volume, low security requirements, and no mission criticality. Public solutions could be better/faster/cheaper than internal provisioning.

Thus, our cloud strategy is to create private clouds that are more reliable, more secure, and cheaper than public clouds for those applications which require higher levels of availability and privacy. For those use cases where the public cloud is good enough, we're considering external solutions.

Someday, it may make sense to move more into the public cloud, but for now, we have the best balance of service, security, and price with a largely private cloud approach.

LIFE AS A HEALTHCARE CIO: Should we abandon the cloud? (May 16 2011 post)

2011 was a bad year for the cloud.

First there was the major Amazon EC2 (Elastic Cloud) outage April 21-22 that brought down many business and websites. Some of the data was unrecoverable and transactions were lost.

Next, the May 10-13 outage of Microsoft's cloud based email and Office services (Business Productivity Online Suite) caused major angst among its customers who thought that the cloud offered increased reliability

Then we had the May 11-13 Google Blogger outage which brought down editing, commenting, and content for thousands of blogs.

Outages from the 3 largest providers of cloud services within a 2 week period does not bode well.

Yesterday, Twitter went down as well.

Many have suggested we abandon a cloud only strategy.

Should we abandon the cloud for healthcare? Absolutely not.

Should we reset our expectations that highly reliable, secure computing can be provided at very low cost by "top men" in the cloud? Absolutely yes.

I am a cloud provider. At my Harvard Medical School Data Center, I provide 4000 Cores and 2 petabytes of data to thousands of faculty and staff. At BIDMC, I provide 500 virtualized servers and a petabyte of data to 12,000 users. Our BIDPO/BIDMC Community EHR Private Cloud provides electronic health records to 300 providers.

I know what it takes to provide 99.999% uptime. Multiple redundant data centers, clustered servers, arrays of tiered storage, and extraordinary power engineering.

With all of this amazing infrastructure comes complexity. With complexity comes unanticipated consequences, change control challenges, and human causes of failure.

Let's look at the downtime I've had this year.

1. BIDMC has a highly redundant, geographically dispersed Domain Name System (DNS) architecture. It theory it should not be able to fail. In practice it did. The vendor was attempting to add features that would make us even more resilient. Instead of making changes to a test DNS appliance, they accidentally made changes to a production DNS appliance. We experienced downtime in several of our applications.

2. HMS has clustered thousands of computing cores together to create a highly robust community resource connected to a petabyte of distributed storage nodes. In theory is should be invincible. In practice it went down. A user with limited high performance computing experience launched a poorly written job to 400 cores in parallel that caused a core dump every second contending for the same disk space. Storage was overwhelmed and went offline for numerous applications.

3. BIDMC has a highly available cluster to support clinical applications. We've upgraded to the most advanced and feature rich Linux operating system. Unfortunately, it had a bug that when used in a very high performance clustered environment, the entire storage file system became unavailable. We had downtime.

4. BIDMC has one of the most sophisticated power management systems in the industry - every component is redundant. As we added features to make us even more redundant, we needed to temporarily reroute power, which is not an issue for us because every network router and switch has two power supplies. We had competed 4 of 5 data center switch migrations when the redundant power supply failed on the 5th switch, bringing down several applications.

5. The BIDPO EHR hosting center has a highly redundant and secure network. Unfortunately, bugs in the network operating system on some of the key components led to failure of all traffic to flow.

These examples illustrate that even the most well engineered infrastructure can fail due to human mistakes, operating system bugs, and unanticipated consequences of change.

The cloud is truly no different. Believing that Microsoft, Google, Amazon or anyone else can engineer perfection at low cost is fantasy. Technology is changing so fast and increasing demand requires so much change that every day is like replacing the wings on a 747 while it's flying. On occasion bad things will happen. We need to have robust downtime procedures and business continuity planning to respond to failures when they occur.

The idea of creating big data in the cloud, clusters of processors, and leveraging the internet to support software as a service applications is sound.

There will be problems. New approaches to troubleshooting issues in the cloud will make "diagnosis and treatment" of slowness and downtime faster.

Problems on a centralized cloud architecture that is homogenous, well documented, and highly staffed can be more rapidly resolved than problems in distributed, poorly staffed, one-off installations.

Thus, I'm a believer in the public cloud and private clouds. I will continue to use them for EHRs and other healthcare applications. However, I have no belief that the public cloud will have substantially less downtime or lower cost than I can engineer myself.

The reason to use the public cloud is so that my limited staff can spend their time innovating - creating infrastructure and applications that the public cloud has not yet envisioned or refuses to support because of regulatory requirements (such as HIPAA).

Despite the black cloud of the past two weeks, the future of the cloud, tempered by a dose of reality to reset expectations, is bright.

Appendix to Chapter 11: BYOD should not be "Build Your Own Disaster"

LIFE AS A HEALTHCARE CIO: Bring Your Own Device (October 3 2011 post)

At BIDMC, I oversee 10,600 desktops and 2000 laptops. They are all locked down with System Center Configuration Manager 2007and McAfee ePolicy Orchestrator.

Given that most of our applications are thin client and web-based, we can stretch the lifetimes of our desktops to 5-6 years and our laptops to 3-4 years. Capital funding puts limits on how much hardware we can buy and how long we keep it.

Like many IT departments, we have to balance many priorities - security, cost, software compatibility, performance and the user experience.

This balance means that the locked down, image managed, economical device provided by the IT department will almost always be older, lower powered, and less capable than the device in your home.

The same is true of mobile devices like Blackberries which are a one time purchase and are only replaced when they stop functioning.

Consumer devices are more than just technology, they've become lifestyle accessories. Are you an iPad2 or a Macbook Air 11 person? Does Android tickle your fancy or are you holding out for the Samsung tablet with Windows 8?

The cost of these devices is low enough that consumers can buy them on their own and may upgrade yearly as new models are released.

All of this has led to the BYOD movement - Device to *work.*

One of my passions as a CIO has been to create web-based applications that run anywhere on anything. That approach has enabled our applications to run on every version of the iPad, iPhone and iPod touch as well as Android and Blackberry devices like the Playbook.

However, I'm also accountable for the privacy and security of each byte of person identified data and we have over 1.5 petabytes to protect.

The internet is an increasingly hostile place. Clicking on a picture of Heidi Klum results in a 1 in 10 chance that your device will become infected.

Online apps distributed via social networks are filled will malware.

Hacked websites can bring malware onto our device. A CIO at the recent Information Week 500 conference described that hackers inserted malware, which was only one pixel by one pixel, into a public-facing website his lab supported. All internal users who browsed to the website and did not have the latest version of Adobe Flash were infected. Once infected, their workstations scanned for other vulnerabilities on the network.

Breach reporting regulations in HITECH are strict. If a keystroke logger embedded in malware results in username/password compromise and a hacker downloads files or views data for more than 500 people, the prominent media needs to be notified. It is unlikely that the media will see much difference between an infected personal device and something under the CIO's control - the CIO will be held accountable!

BIDMC has over 1000 iPads and over 1600 iPhones accessing its network for email and web applications. I absolutely see the value of the Bring Your Own Device movement.

However, the compliance and regulatory requirements that grow more complex every day make the BYOD movement very problematic.

It may be that we'll find some compromise, such as encouraging BYOD, noting that little support will be available, and requiring mobile device security solutions such as Good Technologies before a personal device is allowed on the network.

BYOD can be empowering to users. Let's hope we can mitigate the risk and afford the applications needed to comply with federal and state laws.

LIFE AS A HEALTHCARE CIO: The BIDMC Laptop Encryption Program (July 23 2012 post)

I've been writing about the Bring Your Own Device (BYOD)/Consumer IT challenge for the past several months. Here's the message we sent to employees:

"Information Systems will be conducting an aggressive campaign to ensure every mobile device is encrypted. This initiative applies to all staff and students. The program is mandatory and required for any mobile device used to access BIDMC-related systems, programs or documents, including email, clinical applications and administrative documents such as financial spreadsheets, grant information or staff lists.

Many of you participated in last month's program regarding smart phone devices used to connect to the Exchange email system using ActiveSync. These devices now require password protection. Look for more information soon on new smartphone encryption and 'auto wipe' requirements.

Securing Laptops and iPads

The next stage of work is encrypting laptops, iPads and other tablet computers. It will proceed in two phases.

The first phase, beginning this week, focuses on institutionally owned laptops and iPad-type tablet computers. Other versions of tablet computers will be addressed in a later phase. Service depots will be set up in and around the main campus. The first location will be the Center for Life Sciences (CLS). This building was chosen because it has the largest population of laptops and iPads.

We appreciate the cooperation of staff of CLS especially because you are the first to undergo this new process. The CLS experience will guide IS planning for the entire medical center. We will *coordinate our encryption program with Research Administration's research equipment inventory project, eliminating redundant phone calls to investigators.*

What You Need to Do

Prepare Your Device – Prior to dropping off the laptop or iPad at the service depot, delete unneeded applications and data. All valuable data and important files, email, applications and other documents stored on the device should be backed up to your network home directory. Do NOT back up the data to an Internet cloud service such as Apple's iCloud, or DropBox. Storing protected health or personal information on these sites is against corporate security policy.

Schedule an Appointment - Information Systems will contact staff for which records show you have been issued an institutionally funded laptop or iPad.

Leave the Device - Encrypting a device may require several hours depending on the method used. For this reason, you will be expected to leave the device at the service depot. Every attempt will be made to complete the work within the same business day.

Pick Up the Device - Upon returning the device, depot staff will brief you on what work was done and your on-going responsibilities for maintaining the security of the device. You will be asked to start the device from a cold boot and verify it is in working order.

What IS Will Do

Intake – To qualify under HIPAA/HITECH 'safe harbor', full disk encryption is required. On arrival at the service depot, an initial assessment of the device's configuration will be done to determine the most appropriate encryption method, e.g. software or hardware based. Some devices have encryption built in, but it needs to be activated. The method used will depend on the make, model and operating system version of the laptop or tablet computer.

Inspection - The service depot staff will scan the device for malware and vulnerabilities. They will check configuration settings to assure they comply with corporate security policy such as power-on password, inactivity timeouts, and, for iPads, auto wipe. If time permits, depot staff will apply operating system and third party software patches necessary to eliminate security vulnerabilities. If malware is detected, the device will be cleaned or re-imaged depending on the nature of the malware. The network address of the device will be recorded so I.S. knows it has been inspected when it appears on the data network. When practical, management (Microsoft SCCM for Windows or Casper for Macs) and anti-virus agents (McAfee EPO) will be installed to allow Information Systems staff to keep the device in good security hygiene throughout its life while in use at BIDMC.

Inventory the Device for Research – If your computer is one that still needs to be scanned as part of the bi-annual Research inventory required by federal law, a member of the Research Administration staff will scan the inventory tag while it is at the depot – or apply an inventory tag as needed. We are combining these efforts to make it more convenient for users.

Return - See #4 above.

What is Next?
The dates and locations for other service depot sites will be announced later this month as IS continues to secure laptops and iPads throughout the medical center.

The second phase will extend the program to other models of institutionally owned tablet computers as well as personally owned laptops and tablet computers that are used to access BIDMC-related data. This phase will begin in the fall after work *on institutionally owned devices is completed. We will assist in encrypting and, time permitting, patching the devices. Once done, it will be the responsibility of the owner to maintain the encryption and healthy state of the device.*

Information Systems will periodically check your mobile device to ensure the safeguards are still in place. Additionally, staff must attest, each time their password is renewed, that all mobile devices they use for hospital related business, including personal devices, are encrypted.

From this point forward, newly acquired laptop and tablet computers purchased from institutional funds cannot be used to access the BIDMC data network until their encryption status is verified by Information Systems.

Information Systems will monitor the network for rogue laptop and tablet devices that have not been screened for compliance. If a device is discovered that has not been screened, Internet access privileges will be blocked."

As I've told the press, it is no longer sufficient to rely on policy alone to secure personal mobile devices. Institutions must educate their staff, assist them with encryption, and in some cases purchase software/hardware for personal users to ensure compliance with Federal and State regulations. Over the next few months, I'll write several posts about our lessons learned supporting personal device security enhancements.

Appendix to Chapter 15: What a CIO needs to survive is a high performing team

LIFE AS A HEALTHCARE CIO: Characteristics of high performing teams (August 2 2011 post)

I've written previously about those times in my career when alignment of leadership and resources led to major achievements. High performing teams are a pre-requisite to such achievement and here are a few characteristics of high performing teams I have worked with:

Competence
Domain expertise and an ability to execute assigned tasks are key to ensuring vision is turned into successful implementation. My experience is that "A" players hire "A" players and "B" players hire "C" players. This means that highly competent people surround themselves with skilled people because they do not feel intimated by having subordinates or colleagues who are smarter, more talented, or more successful. No member of a team can do everything, so having a group of smart people working together creates a sum greater than the parts. On the other hand, incompetent people tend to hire even less competent people to shore up their own egos and self image. Leaders need to be very careful when retaining marginally performing teams, because incompetent people hiring less competent people can get the organization in trouble very quickly.

Trust
As a rock climber, I know that my life depends upon the skill and decision making of my climbing partner. No matter how good I am, a mistake by my partner could kill both of us. Every day I think about my teams and ask if I would trust them to hold my rope. A high performing team requires a level of trust and confidence that fosters a joy of collective achievement rather than fear of individual failure. Creating an environment of trust has worked for me as a parent and is an essential part of an

optimized team.

Communication
I realize that carrying mobile devices creates the burden of being connected 24 hours a day. I do not inflict my own work schedule on any of my teams (my last true day off was in the summer of 1984). However, creating a level of communication among team members that enables rapid escalation and resolution of issues is essential to high performance. Teams should respect the need for time away but arrange coverage such that email, instant messaging, paging, phone calls, and web-based collaboration can be initiated at a moment's notice for resolution of complex issues that are often precipitated by circumstances beyond the control of the team. Teams should create a level of transparency that keeps all members informed of current priorities, strategies, and challenges using blogs, wikis, and meetings (to the extent necessary). Great communication reduces friction, enhances decision making, and reduces unnecessary work.

Loyalty
Highly functional team members are always there for each other. No matter what happens, they do not throw their colleagues under the bus. They give an early heads up when projects or staff members are in trouble. They accelerate decision making by contributing positively to consensus building. They respect hierarchical boundaries, escalating problems by collaborating with team leaders and managers. The result is a team that is deeply loyal to its members rather than focused on highlighting the success of any one individual.

The Greater Good
In my trip to Japan, I discussed priority setting in the Japanese bureaucracy. At times it appears that ministries set priorities based on sustaining their own power and authority. Bureaus within ministries can set priorities in silos. Rarely is the greater good for the country the driving force that unifies budgeting at every level. Highly functional teams think about the overall

goals of the organization and craft their plans around those activities which will create the greatest good for the greatest number. There is not siloed thinking about resources, budgets, or achieving individual goals at the expense of team of goals.

High performing teams are hard to create and sustain, but when they happen, they are to be treasured. There is nothing I will not do for my high performing teams.

Appendix to Chapter 17: Lessons about "IT Governance & Communication" by an outstanding CIO leader

LIFE AS AN HEALTHCARE CIO: It is not a Job, it's a Lifestyle (November 2 2007 post)

I'm often asked, "What is your job?"

Some may think that being a CIO is all about bits and bytes, buying the latest technology and keeping up with all the three letter acronyms of the industry (I use WPA over EAP instead of WEP on my wireless network, what do you use?).

The technology portion of my job is about 15% of my time. The bulk of what I do is organizational, political, and customer relationship management. With hundreds of projects, thousands of customers, and millions of dollars, how do I keep it all straight?

My approach is 4 fold:

1. Strategy - The Information Technology department in every organization should not make the business strategy, that is up to the Board, CEO, and stakeholders. The IT organization should provide the tactics necessary to execute the organization's strategic plan. For example, if the strategy is to improve quality, the information technology organization can implement e-Prescribing, provider order entry, bar coded wrist bands, and incident tracking systems. Every year, I approach the strategic planning process by meeting with the CEO, CFO, COO, Chief Medical Officer, Chief Nursing Officer, and Chief Academic Officer to understand their strategic imperatives for the year. The next month, I meet with their direct reports to understand the operational implications and challenges of these strategic imperatives. I then produce an "IS Operating Plan" (note, that it is not a strategic plan), which is placed on the web for all stakeholders to review and presented to my IS Steering Committees. I have a Steering Committee for inpatient applications, outpatient applications, critical care applications, Operating Room/Anesthesia, Laboratory systems, Radiology systems, and Health Information Management (Medical Records). The chairs of each of these committees plus clinician representatives from the Medical Executive Committee serve on the enterprise wide Information Systems Steering Committee which ensures coordination of resources among all the projects. Once these committees approve the priorities for the year, we ensure the operating and capital budgets are aligned to do the work.

2. Structure - Once the operating plan is in place, I ensure the structure of the organization is arranged to support the projects to be done. Over the past 10 years I've done several mini-reorganizations to respond to changing technologies, customer needs, and governance issues. Note that the ideal structure is defined before taking into account the existing staff personalities and skillsets. To build an organization that delivers reliable service over time, I try to avoid single points of human failure, distributing work across many individuals rather than relying on a "lone genius", since reliance on one person is ultimately unsupportable.

3. Staffing - Once the structure is in place, I ensure we have the best staff possible to populate that structure. I'm a strong believer in training and we try our best, given limited budgets, to hire talented people and continue their education so they remain world class experts. I'm also a great supporter of co-op programs for college students, bringing in new graduates, training them and hiring them to ensure a constant supply of new talent entering the organization.

4. Processes - Finally, once the staffing is in place, I work on the highly repeatable processes that support our workflow. The organization functions most smoothly when policies and procedures are well known by all internal and external to the organization so that I can monitor the performance of known processes, rapidly identifying areas where we can improve service delivery. Metrics I review include infrastructure uptime, electrical consumption, help desk call abandonment rates/time to problem resolution, budget performance by manager, and performance against project timeline milestones.

At the beginning of each day, I ask myself if the strategy, structure, staffing and processes are as good as they can be. At the end of each day, I mentally review the issues of the day affecting each of my direct reports and offer mid course corrections, which are most often organizational and political. I also try to communicate broadly via town meetings, email broadcasts, weekly leadership meetings, and monthly 1:1 meetings with each of my direct reports.

Finally, I try to reserve 50% of my time each day for the important issues of that day. Explaining to a customer or IS employee that I cannot respond to a critical issue for weeks because my calendar is booked far in advance does not work. If I can do today's work today, my calendar has the same number of meetings, but I become a real time responder to issues before they escalate. Having a Blackberry strapped to my belt 21 hours a day also helps me use my time efficiently and ensures I am not the rate limiting step in any decision-making process.

Of course I have a family life, personal time and outside interests, but being a CIO is a lifestyle, not a job. I'm connected to the strategy, structure, staffing and processes of the organization 24x7x365.

LIFE AS AN HEALTHCARE CIO: The Tyranny of the Urgent (November 11 2007 post)

Providing cutting edge clinical applications to a hospital is journey. It requires daily efforts to refine workflow and encourage adoption but it also requires a multiyear plan to ensure future needs will be met. Three years ago, it was clear that e-Prescribing would be very important. However in 2004, faxing to retail pharmacies was all we had. Today, with the Surescripts connection to retail pharmacies and the RxHub connection to mail order pharmacies, we have fully electronic transmission for 90% of our prescriptions. The only way we were able to support all aspects of e-Prescribing including formulary enforcement, eligibility checking, community drug history with drug/drug interactions, and prescription routing was to focus a portion of each day on our long term goals without being derailed by each day's distractions.

I call the distractions of each day, "the tyranny of the urgent". Everyone believes that long term goals like medication safety are essential, but each day some stakeholder has a new, mission critical project that is expected to trump existing priorities. Of course there are legitimate urgent projects that must be done for quality, safety, compliance or return on investment, but if we allowed every project proposed each day to defer our multi-year plan, we'd never accomplish our long term goals.

Thus, I spend 50% of my day on email, phone calls and the tyranny of the urgent, but reserve 50% of each day for those projects which will create revolutionary change three years from now. To do so requires two kinds of plans.

My Operating Plan outlines the goals of each year - ensuring that each business owner's strategic priorities are met on a yearly basis. To ensure stakeholders understand the major themes of our yearly operating plan, I produce a thematic summary.

I also have a 5 year plan which outlines the "big picture" so that all stakeholders know where we're going year to year. Of course I watch for major industry trends and refine the 5 year plan in response to changes in technology, legislation and compliance requirements, but in general, the 5 year plan is a predictable roadmap of what we'll accomplish over the long term.

Many days, it feels like my job is driven by the contents of my Inbox, but in order to create a successful organization, I have to insulate my staff from attempts to change priorities on a daily basis. Instead, my job is to triage the entropy of my inbox into a few short term urgencies while protecting the operating plan and five year plan. At times, this triage exercise is challenging and I involve my various governance committees when decisions are politically charged or involving competing stakeholder priorities.

My advice to CIOs is to develop standard escalation processes and use those well defined processes each day in response to the tyranny of the urgent. Do not let your inbox dictate your strategy or priorities. Keep your eye on the big picture. As Jim Barksdale says, "The main thing is to make the main thing the main thing."

LIFE AS AN HEALTHCARE CIO: How to say "No" (November 19 2007 post)

I was recently asked to give a lecture about how I say "no" to new project requests. Of course I have governance committees which help prioritize all IT projects based on

Return on Investment
Quality/Compliance
Impact factor - number of doctors, nurses, staff and patients who will benefit
Alignment with the strategic needs of the business

Beyond my governance processes, which I will describe further in another post, my top 10 list of how to say "no" is more about people than prioritization.

10. Select your change (and what not to change)
I've learned that my hospital organization (BIDMC) does not readily accept off the shelf enterprise application software. In the past decade, we've stopped a major clinical and a major revenue cycle project because of the limited customization possibilities with vendor supplied software. To this day, our self-built customized enterprise applications keep customers happy at low cost. Of course I still buy many departmental systems (lab, critical care, anesthesia, labor and deliver monitoring, PACS, cardiology) but will no longer try to replace our enterprise clinical applications with vendor products. This is an automatic "no" that customers understand.

9. Identify those who will lose and take them to lunch
On a given day, 10% of the organization is not completely satisfied with the triage decisions made by my governance committees. In a world of limited supply and infinite demand, the organization needs to say "no" to many projects. I find that bad news does not travel well via email, hence personal contact is needed to explain many prioritization decisions. I try to make

personal contact with those whose projects are not funded/prioritized. Whenever possible, instead of "never", I say "not now" to lower priority projects.

8. Acknowledge the loss
Many people will accept change if the process is transparent, they are involved in the decision, and their losses are acknowledged. Telling folks that you understand the impact of negative decisions and expressing a willingness to work together in the future goes a long way.

7. Over Communicate
Rumors are often worse than the truth. Every Friday I send out a broadcast email to the entire organization explaining issues, good news, bad news, and future plans.

6. Be Honest and Consistent
I work hard to tell all stakeholders the same message. If everyone hears the good and bad news consistently, the credibility of IT is enhanced.

5. Consensus is not essential
A vote of 500 to 1 is not a tie. If governance works objectively, even politically powerful stakeholders cannot veto prioritization decisions which are in the best interest of the organization.

4. Embrace conflict
Sometimes the right decisions are the hard or politically challenging ones. By expecting conflict every day, the CIO can make decisions more dispassionately. My training as an emergency physician prepared me to approach every situation with balanced emotions. Eliminating caffeine 5 years ago helped too.

3. Focus on your detractors
Sometimes organizations can be 1000 points of veto. By focusing on those who oppose projects instead of those which support

them, I can use my time most effectively. I'd rather meet with my friends, but my day is optimized when I spend the day with my detractors. Sometimes detractors become friends, but at least all detractors understand the rationale for "no" decisions.

2. The last two minutes of the meeting are the most important
It's very common for politically challenging meetings to end with differing opinions as to what was discussed. Using the last two minutes of the meeting to review all the decisions made and next steps, then memorializing that conversation in written minutes, enhances the communication of "no"

1. You cannot please everyone
I accept that the good of the many outweighs the needs of the few, even if I have to be the "no" guy.

LIFE AS AN HEALTHCARE CIO: Time, Scope and Resources (December 4 2007 post)

Recently, the number of new infrastructure project requests has peaked to unprecedented levels. The usual triage mechanisms described in my previous blog entry work well for applications, but infrastructure is different. Adding a new network port, a new telephone, or a new desktop is viewed a service business that can be ordered on demand, making it very challenging to say 'no'.

The sudden surge in requests re-emphasized to me the basic law of all IT projects - timeline, scope and resources are inter-related. If scope increases, timeline or resources must increase. If timeline is shortened, scope must be decreased or resources increased. Increasing scope, shortening timeline while leaving resources constant is not possible.

Of course, we can all work harder. There are 168 hours in a week, vacations can be postponed and nights/weekends filled. This works in the short term, but is not sustainable. "Lean" and "mean" organizations pushed too hard become "bony" and "angry" organizations.

New FTEs are not typically the short term answer. Getting new positions raises expectations of delivery capacity but hiring and training new staff take resources from existing capacity, so paradoxically getting new positions actually reduces capacity for a few months.

This means there is only one short term answer for unplanned, unbudgeted, unscheduled infrastructure requests - the scope of these requests needs to be reduced/phased or the time to do them increased.

For my requests this week, I've done the following
a. Assigned my staff to develop a standard worksheet which outlines the major time limiting steps (i.e. network connections

take 90 days to provision) and thus specifies the minimum lead time for building IS support for a new location
b. Negotiated a change in scope with phasing - the initial request for a high bandwidth connection and new telephone system was morphed into a low bandwidth connection and use of the existing telephone system for now.
c. Reordered priorities - previous request were placed on hold in order to service the new 'once in a lifetime' opportunities
d. Asked for new staff - with the caveat that they will not add to capacity/throughput for 6 months
e. Requested governance changes - to ensure a central committee triages and communicates infrastructure requests for new offsite locations

There is one other strategy that I could employ if this surge in requests becomes chronic. In the past, I've staffed to average work load, not peak workload. This means that staff can put in extra hours for short term urgent increases in demand. However, I may have to staff to peak so that excess capacity is always available for the continuous infrastructure tyranny of the urgent. I'm a frugal guy, doing a great deal on a limited budget, so I've never built in excess capacity.

LIFE AS AN HEALTHCARE CIO: IT Governance (December 31 2007 post)

One of the most important steps a CIO can take to ensure alignment of IT with the business strategy of the organization is to create robust governance committees. It's also the best way for a CIO to satisfy customers, respond to the tyranny of the urgent, and keep the CIO employed!

I've mentioned governance issues in several previous posts:
Time Scope and Resources
How to Say No
Tyranny of the Urgent
It's not a Job it's a Lifestyle

In the interest of transparency, I'd like to describe my governance successes and failures plus my 2008 plans for IT governance.

At Beth Israel Deaconess, I have committees for each of my major groups of IT customers:

- *Laboratory Information Systems co-chaired by the Senior Vice President (SVP) for Operations and the Chief of Pathology (an MD)*
- *Radiology Information Systems co-chaired by the SVP for Operations and the Chief of Radiology (an MD)*
- *Critical Care Information Systems chaired by the Director Trauma, Anesthesia and Critical Care (an MD)*
- *Inpatient Information Systems (includes Provider Order Entry) chaired by the Senior Director of Clinical Resource Management (an MD)*
- *Ambulatory Information Systems chaired by the SVP of Ambulatory & Emergency Services (an RN)*
- *Health Information Management Information Systems chaired by the Director of the Hospital Medicine Program (an MD)*

- *Community Information Systems chaired by the Executive Director of the Physician's Organization and the SVP for Network Development (an MD)*
- *Decision Support Steering Committee chaired by the Director of Business Planning & Decision Support and the SVP for Healthcare Quality (an MD)*
- *Enterprise Resource Planning (ERP) Information Systems chaired by the Director of Business Services and the Controller*
- *Revenue Cycle Information Systems chaired by the Chief Financial Officer*

This structure worked very well for the past 10 years, ensuring that each application had a lifecycle prioritized by the clinicians and not the IT department. However, in 2007, we needed to make a change. As BIDMC grew into a 1.2 billion dollar organization, an emphasis was placed on achieving an operating margin which would yield the capital budgets needed for expansion. This meant that IT budgets did not grow at the same pace as the clinical budgets and led to competition for IT resources among my governance committees. Existing governance committees set the right priorities within each business area, but we did not have a governance construct to set priorities among all the business areas. Thus, we created an overall IT Steering Committee comprised of the chairs of each of the existing governance committees. The terms of reference for this new committee are here.

At Harvard Medical School (HMS), I also have committees for each of my major groups of IT customers:

- *Administrative Information Technology chaired by the Executive Dean for Administration*
- *Educational Applications Committee chaired by the Executive Director of Curriculum Programs*

- *Research Information Technology chaired by the Director of the Research Information Technology Group*

Like BIDMC, these three committees functioned very well over the past 5 years to ensure priorities were set within the domains of the three core businesses of HMS - research, teaching and administration. A new Dean of HMS took office on September 4, 2007 and launched a strategic planning process. The result of this process could be a substantially broader scope for IT, requiring new resources and scalability. Depending on the outcome of the planning processes, IT governance may need to be revised. Harvard University just completed a governance audit of IT departments and the following are the unedited conclusions about Harvard Medical School:

"A school-wide committee overseeing coordination of IT resources among HMS' three primary business groups does not exist. HMS has functioned as three core businesses: research, education and administration. HMS IT has established governance processes for each of these three businesses which have led to a high degree of customer satisfaction.

As the new HMS strategic planning process creates new projects and stakeholders, the individual governance committees will evolve to align with the new strategic needs, including the creation of a school-wide IT Steering Committee if appropriate. There is a risk that IT resources could be allocated inequitably among the three core businesses and decisions made without the involvement of key business stakeholders.

The HMS CIO will participate in HMS strategic planning, identifying and documenting governance requirements and school-wide committee needs to ensure appropriate allocation and prioritization of IT resources by May 1, 2008. "

Thus, there may be a need for an overall IT Steering Committee at HMS. Bigger committees are not always better committees and creating a committee to objectively balance the heterogeneous needs of research, education and administration will be challenging. However, I'm very willing to do it if the demand for resources by any one group of customers significantly conflicts with the requirements of other customers.

A few lessons learned from the governance experience above:

In a hospital, it is key that clinicians (MDs and RNs) run the IT governance committees. You'll note that I do not chair any committee other than serving as co-chair of the overall steering committee. My role in that committee is a facilitator only and I do not vote on priority setting.

It's very important to have governance committees that are focused enough to really grasp the details of stakeholders needs. It may appear that I have too many governance committees, but this is the parsimonious number required to ensure that priorities are set at the application level.

Governance must evolve with the needs of the business. I am a servant of the organizations which employ me and I do not have an agenda of my own. Hence I will gladly change governance as needed to be maximally responsive to changes in the business environment around me.

I want to thank the Harvard Risk Management and Audit Services for their work this Fall which truly enabled me to evaluate the effectiveness of all my IT governance groups.

LIFE AS AN HEALTHCARE CIO: Creating quantitative IT Governance (December 5 2012 post)

Over the past few months I've been talking to many industry leaders about the challenge of matching IT supply and demand. Governance committees are essential but are not enough when the number of project requests is so large that they become difficult to triage.

Objective, quantitative scoring criteria can help.

Intel has implemented a Business Value Index that is based on numerical scoring of

Customer need
Business and technical risks
Strategic fit
Revenue potential
Level of required investment
Amount of innovation and learning generated

My colleagues at Stanford have developed a quantitative approach based on a weighted scoring of

Quality and Effectiveness
User Productivity and Satisfaction (includes providers, patients, referring MDs)
Compliance (required by law or external regulatory/accreditation body)
Patient Safety
Financial
Scope/Urgency

Their process is very robust as described by Dr. Pravene Nath

"We take all inbound requests, whether captured by helpdesk or

in meetings. A clinical informaticist reviews the request and presents it at our scoring committee meeting, which lasts for about an hour each week. The informaticist provides a preliminary scoring, and the group either confirms it, adjusts it, or sends it back for more research. Occasionally a request will be outright denied at the meeting if it just doesn't make sense. We have an appeals process for the requestor but it is rarely used. All requests, regardless of age, are kept in a rank ordered list by priority based on score. The application teams work from the top of that list downward, and they don't pick up anything new from the list until something currently underway is completed. Lastly, we reserve some capacity for fast track (easy items) which can be done even if lower on the list."

BIDMC has prioritized capital projects (IT and others) by scoring

Return on Investment
Strategic Alignment
Impact factor (Employees, Clinicians, Patients)
Quality/Safety
Compliance/Regulatory

We have policies that require CIO sign off of all IT-related projects to ensure grant funded/departmental funded IT projects are prioritized along with institutionally funded capital projects.

This year, we're looking to expand quantitative IT governance to those projects which are not capital funded and simply use existing staff resources.

I welcome your input on approaches you have used to rank project requests in a way that stakeholders feel is objective, transparent, and fair.

LIFE AS AN HEALTHCARE CIO: Authority, Responsibility, and Risk (September 15 2011 post)

When I became CIO of CareGroup/BIDMC in 1998, I promised to listen to all my staff and collaboratively embrace technologies that would benefit patients while also enabling employee career growth. The IT team worked together to implement new infrastructure and new applications. Success led to an upward spiral of success. Other groups such as Media Services, Knowledge Services, and Health Information Management joined IS. We continued to grow in scope and capability.

My sense at the time was that additional authority, budget and span of control were great - more was better.

However, in my nearly 15 years as CIO, I've learned that while more authority may bring more opportunities to succeed, it also brings increased responsibility and with it, additional risk.

In a world of increasing regulatory pressures and compliance requirements, the likelihood of something bad happening every day in a large organization is high.   The larger your role, the larger your risk.

Today in my BIDMC role I oversee

83 locations
18000 user accounts
9000 desktops/laptops/tablets
3000 printers
600 iPads
1600 iPhones
450 servers (200 physical, 250 virtual)
1.5 petabytes of storage

serving over a million patients.

If one employee copies data to a USB drive and loses it, a potential breach needs to be reported. If one workstation is infected with malware that could have transmitted clinical data to a third party, a potential breach needs to be reported. If one business associate loses an unencrypted laptop, a breach needs to be reported. 30,750 such breaches have been reported since HITECH took effect All breaches are the CIO's responsibility.

If one IT project is over time or over budget, it's the CIO's responsibility.

If one IT employee goes rogue, it's the CIO's responsibility.

If one server, network, or storage array fails, it's the CIO's responsibility

If one application causes patient harm, it's the CIO's responsibility

Life as a CIO can have its challenges!

At the same time that responsibilities are expanding, the number of auditors, regulators, lawyers, compliance specialists, and complex regulations is growing at a much faster rate than IT resources.

There are three solutions

1. Spend increasing amounts of time on risk identification and mitigation
2. Reduce your responsibility/accountability and thus your risk footprint
3. Find a nice cabin in the woods and homestead as far away from regulatory burdens as possible

I'm doing #1 - about 20% of my day is spent on matters of risk, compliance, and regulation. I'm doing #2 by transitioning my CIO role at Harvard Medical School to a successor. #3 sounds appealing but I'm not there yet!

As healthcare CIOs face new regulations for e-prescribing of controlled substances, FDA device safety requirements, 5010 implementation, ICD-10, new privacy rules, and Meaningful Use stages 1-2-3, the magnitude of the challenges ahead may at times seem overwhelming. I sometimes long for the days when all I had to do was write innovative software and create a nurturing environment for my staff!

There are 3 negative consequences that can result from overzealous regulation:

1. The joy of success can turn into a fear of compliance failure
2. Compliance can create such overhead that we lose our competitiveness
3. We'll become less entrepreneurial because the consequences of non-compliance, such as loss of reputation, penalties, and burden of responding to agencies enforcing regulations, become a deterrent to innovation.

For now, I have accepted the risks that come with all my responsibilities, but at some point, the balance may become more challenging to maintain. As we move forward, I hope that policymakers in Washington and at the state level will be mindful of the unintended consequences of regulatory complexity.

LIFE AS AN HEALTHCARE CIO: How to be a bad CIO (February 26 2008 post)

In my decade as a CIO, I've seen a lot of turnover in the IT industry. Each time a CIO is fired, I've asked around to learn about the root cause. Here's my list of the top 10 ways to be a bad CIO.

1. Start each meeting with a chip on your shoulder
Human nature is such that every organization has politics and conflicts. Sometimes these differences of opinion lead to emotional email or confrontational meetings. If the CIO develops an attitude that presupposes every request will be unreasonable and every interaction unpleasant, then every meeting will become unproductive. I find that listening to naysayers, understanding common ground, and developing a path forward works with even the most difficult customers. Instead of believing that meetings with challenging customers will be negative, I think of them as opportunities for a "walk in the woods"

2. Bypass governance processes and set priorities yourself
Although it's true that some budget decisions must be made by the CIO, such as maintaining infrastructure, the priorities for application development should be based on customer driven Governance Committees . Even the best of intentions can lead to a mismatch between customer expectations and IT resource allocation. I recently participated in a meeting to discuss technology problems, when in fact the problem was governance - a lack of communication among the stakeholders, resulting in unclear priorities and unmet expectations. Once the governance is clarified and communication channels established, IT can deliver on customer priorities and meet expectations.

3. Protect your staff at the expense of customer and institutional needs
As a CIO, I work hard to prevent my 'lean and mean' staff from becoming 'bony and angry'. However, I also work with the

customers to balance resources, scope and timing, rather than just saying 'no'. Sometimes organizational priorities will be overwhelming due to sudden compliance issues or "must do" strategic opportunities. I do my best to redirect resources to these new priorities, explaining that existing projects will slow down. My attitude is that I do not know the end of play in the middle of Act I, so I cannot really understand the impact of new priority initiatives until I accept their positive possibilities and start working on the details. Tolerate some ambiguity, accept change, support the institution and if a resource problem evolves, then ask for help.

4. *Put yourself first*
I've written that life as a CIO is a lifestyle, not a job. Weekends and nights are filled with system upgrades. Pagers and cell phones go off at inopportune moments. Vacations and downtime are a balance with operational responsibilities. When I go on vacation, I get up an hour before my family, catch up on email, then spend the day with my family. At night, I go to bed an hour after they do, catching up on the day's events. It's far worse to ignore email and phone calls for a week then come back to a desk filled with loose ends. Being a CIO requires a constant balance of personal and professional time.

5. *Use mutually assured destruction negotiating tactics*
Walking into the CEO's office and saying that you will quit unless your budget is increased does not win the war. It may result in temporary victory but it demeans the CIO. Similarly, telling customers that the CEO, COO and CFO are to be blamed for lack of resources does not make the organization look good. The CIO should be a member of senior management and all resource decisions should be made together by consensus, even if the outcome is not always positive for IT.

6. *Hide your mistakes/undercommunicate*
My network outage in 2002 resulted in what was called "the worst IT disaster in healthcare history". By sharing all my lessons

learned with the press and internal customers, everyone understood the combination of issues and events that caused the problem. I received email from CIOs all over the world explaining their similar problems that had been hidden due to PR concerns. I have found that transparency and overcommunication may be challenging in the short term, but always improves the situation in the long term.

7. Burn Bridges
It's a small world and the best policy is to be as cordial and professional as possible with every stakeholder, even your worst naysayers. A dozen years ago before I was CIO, I presented to the IT steering committee about the need to embrace the web. I was told by a senior IT leader that they did not care what I had to say since I was not an important stakeholder. A year later, I became CIO and that IT senior leader left the organization within a week.

8. Don't give your stakeholders a voice
Sitting in your office and not meeting with customers is doom for the CIO. Every day, I fill my schedule with meetings in the trenches with all the stakeholders to understand what is working and what is not. I never shoot the messenger when I'm told that our products or services need improvement. A CIO can earn a lot of respect just by listening to the honest feedback from every part of the organization.

9. Embrace obsolete technologies
The CIO should never be the rate limiting step for adoption of new technologies and ideas. If Open Source, Apple products, and Web 2.0 are the way is world going, the CIO should be the first in line to test them.

10. Think inside the box
Facebook as a Rapid Application Development platform? Empowering users to do self service data mining? Piloting thin client devices and flexible work arrangements? Although exploring new ideas will not always result in a breakthrough, it's

much more likely to create innovation than maintain the status quo.

Each time you approach a senior manager, a customer or an employee, remind yourself of the top 10 ways to be a bad CIO. By avoiding these behaviors, you may find yourself embraced by the organization for many years to come.

LIFE AS AN HEALTHCARE CIO: New metrics for CIO success (November 1 2011 post)

When I begin my career as a CIO in 1997, success was function of the basics - email delivery, network connectivity, and application functionality. I personally wrote code, experimented with new operating systems, and created analytics using web servers, SQL, and ASP pages.

In 2011, CIO success is much more complex to measure.

Infrastructure success can be defined as 99.99% uptime of all systems and no loss/corruption/breach of data. The magical belief in the cloud sets expectations that IT infrastructure should be like heat, power, and light - just there as a utility whenever it is needed in whatever amount is needed.

Application success could be defined as on time, on budget delivery of go lives according to project plans. Two important forces make this more complex
*Consumer software stores set expectations that enterprise software should be easy - we need to fix revenue cycle workflow, isn't there an app for that?
*As the economy forces downsizing and efficiency gains, there's an expectation that workflow automation is a pre-requisite to organizational change so there is more pressure on the IT department to deliver application solutions quickly.

This all sounds impossible - deliver massive infrastructure with constant change but keep it entirely reliable and secure. Deliver applications that support business processes in increasingly short timeframes with limited IT and business owner resources.

Thus, the modern CIO is no longer a technologist or evangelist for innovation. The modern CIO is a customer relationship manager, a strategic communicator, and a project manager, delicately balancing project portfolios, available resources, and *governance.*

Modern CIOs have little time to get infrastructure and applications right, so they must "skate where the puck will be", thinking more like CEOs about business needs and future strategies, so that critical information technology is deployed by the time it is needed.

What am I doing in FY12 to become a more effective modern CIO?

1. I've defined key business customers (BIDMC senior management and chiefs). I'm meeting with each one to ensure their priorities for the next year and beyond are reflected in the FY12 IT operating plan and the 5 year IT strategic plan. Planning much more than 5 years in IT is problematic given the pace of technology change. Working with the governance committees, I will trim this list into those projects that have the greatest impact on business strategy, quality/safety, and efficiency.

2. I'm standardizing communication so that key customers receive monthly updates about their priority projects.

3. I'm defining a process for managing IT projects across the enterprise that includes standardizing the IT Project Intake Process, the IT Project Life-cycle, and Project Management tools (project documentation, project plans, and status reports).

It's my hope that by focusing on customer relationship management, communication and project management that I will create a positive working environment for the IT staff with a more limited set of well-defined projects and more engaged customers.
   Doing fewer projects with greater speed and depth which meet the most critical needs of the business is much harder than agreeing to do many niche projects and moving forward slowly on all. Given that the supply of IT resources is likely to be fixed

since healthcare budgets are under increasing pressure from healthcare reform, the modern CIO should be judged on demand management and achieving reasonable levels of customer satisfaction despite having to focus on a narrower project portfolio delivered at a faster pace.

LIFE AS AN HEALTHCARE CIO: New and Improved (May 7 2008 post)

CIOs rarely receive credit for keeping the trains running on time. Instead, they receive credit for implementing new applications and cool infrastructure features. The challenge is that 80% of IT resources are needed to maintain existing applications and infrastructure, leaving 20% of the total IT budget to be spent on new work. When you consider the multi-year larger projects, the must do compliance issues, and the tyranny of the urgent, there is very little left over to focus on discretionary innovation.

A cutting edge application can rapidly become a legacy system if the stakeholders feel that IT has lost the ability to respond to the needs of the users. What is the best strategy to keep the users happy and make the organization feel that IT is constantly innovating? Here's my approach:

Establish Strong Governance
Governance committees have three major purposes. They provide a process for prioritizing new requests, they establish a team of champions for the application, and they provide a forum for education about an application's features and benefits. Whenever I hear that an application is non-intuitive, has ceased to be innovative or lacks critical features, most of the time it's a governance problem. Do not replace the application, establish a multi-stakeholder governance committee as your first step.

Implement small continuous improvements instead of big bang new applications
A few times in the history of my organizations, stakeholders outside of IT have decided that wholesale replacement of applications or massive new implementations will solve workflow issues. In each case, the issues turned out to be non-IT process problems or weak governance caused by internal politics. The problem with big bang new applications is that they consume all available IT resources and often require existing applications to

be frozen for months (if not years) while the new implementation progresses. Lack of progress in existing applications causes even more frustration and by the time the new application is ready, it's common that needs have changed and the new application is no longer the nirvana it was once thought to be. Making constant small changes in response to constantly evolving customer needs is the best way to achieve satisfaction.

Communicate broadly
For the past decade, I've written an email to everyone in the organization at least once a month describing the latest in IT innovations. With the increase in sensitivity to Spam and broadcast email, I've replaced that communication with blogging. My recent blogs about Integrating the Medical Record, Providing Decision Support, and Clinical Documentation were all in response to internal customer questions about strategy, new features, and priorities. I use blogs, emails, and in person presentations to celebrate IT successes and to educate naysayers.

Enhance the user interface
Just as many people are attracted to new car models because of changes in style or color, users find a new user interface to be a sign of innovation. Especially with the web, it's important to evolve user interfaces to embrace a modern look and feel. The late 1990's were about lists of links. The early 2000's were about graphical elements and color. The mid 2000's were about clean interfaces with blues and whites. 2008 is about pastels, brushed steel, and effective use of screen real estate. All my organizations are now implementing modern 2008 looks to our internal and external web applications.

Run Focus groups and do surveys
As a corollary to governance, it's important to get feedback from the trenches. Doing usability testing with Focus groups and getting candid feedback from a large number of stakeholders via surveys is an effective way to measure the pulse of the organization. When I get detailed feedback, I often find that the

issues which are most bothersome to users are the easiest to fix, such as relabeling a button, changing a screen layout or improving workflow through refinement of a minor feature.

Thus, continuous incremental improvement driven by strong governance is the path to success. For me, 2008, has been more about people than technology. My governance groups are stronger than ever and the buzz is that "New and Improved" applications are rolling out faster than ever.

LIFE AS AN HEALTHCARE CIO: The Year of Governance (October 20 2010 post)

If my epitaph had to be written tomorrow, what pithy quote would I select from my blog?

Possibilities include:
"For everything there is a process"
"The happiest stage of life is wherever I am today"
"The nice guy can finish first"

However, for 2011, I'd suggest "Governance is the solution to all your problems".

I've committed to make 2011 the year of Governance. At Harvard Medical School, we're expanding our Governance Committees to ensure administration, education, and research stakeholders have governance committees which roll up to an executive governance committee of the individual committee chairs. Together, these committees will set the departmental and overall IT priorities for the school.

At BIDMC, we've created a new overall IT Governance Committee in addition to the existing subcommittees that prioritize departmentally focused efforts:

*Laboratory Information Systems chaired by the SVP/VP overseeing the lab
*Radiology Information Systems chaired by the SVP/VP overseeing radiology
*Enterprise Image Management chaired by the CIO
*Emergency Department Information Systems chaired by the SVP overseeing Ambulatory & Emergency Services
*Critical Care Information Systems chaired by the Director Trauma, Anesthesia and Critical Care
*Peri-operative Information Systems chaired by the Director of Perioperative Service

*Inpatient Clinical Applications (includes Provider Order Entry) co-chaired by Chief Nursing Officer and VP for Clinical Systems
*Ambulatory (WebOM) users group chaired by the SVP overseeing Ambulatory & Emergency Services
*Health Information Management Information Systems chaired by the Director of the Hospital Medicine Program
*Community Information Systems chaired by the Executive Director of the Physician's Organization
*Decision Support Steering Committee chaired by the Director of Business Planning & Decision Support and the Vice Chair of General Medicine
*Enterprise Resource Planning (ERP) Information Systems chaired by the Director of Business Services and the Controller
*Human Resources Information Systems chaired by the SVP of Human Resources

The role of the overall IT Governance Committee includes:
*Communication about prioritization and resource decisions.
*Articulating, prioritizing, and monitoring the overall vision for IT at BIDMC.
*Achieving the right balance between built and bought systems including adequate staffing for maintenance to ensure high customer satisfaction.

Why is governance so important for BIDMC in 2011?
*2011 is the most stressful time in the entire history of healthcare IT in the US. Certification and Meaningful Use requires significant application, infrastructure, and change management efforts.
*2011 is the time to begin planning for healthcare reform and the new world of accountable care organizations and the electronic systems we'll need for the future.
*2011 is a time of many new regulatory/compliance mandates including planning for ICD-10, new data protection regulations, and increasing oversight from the Joint Commission/CMS/FDA etc.

LIFE AS AN HEALTHCARE CIO: Leading Change (December 5 2007 post)

Ten years ago this week, I became CIO of CareGroup. On that day, I learned an important lesson about leading change.

Just hours after getting the job I decided that we'd embrace a service oriented architecture (SOA), standardize all desktop/server/storage infrastructure, and implement centrally managed applications. At 8am the next morning, I was scheduled to meet with my 300 staff members and share with them my vision for the future.

Luckily, experienced leaders counseled me on that first day. I discussed my vision with three Board members - Warren McFarlan (Professor at Harvard Business School), John Keane Sr. (CEO of Keane Inc.) and Sam Fleming (CEO of DRI/McGraw Hill). They told me that announcing a strategic plan without engaging all the stakeholders in the process would lead to mixed support and adoption.

Instead of arriving at the 8am meeting with all the answers, I arrived with questions. I explained to the staff that we wanted to improve customer service, encourage innovation, and ensure our work was aligned with the needs of our stakeholders. I challenged them to tell me what they thought we should do. In the first 30 days of my CIO tenure, I met with every staff member in IS as well as every senior manager in CareGroup to gather their priority lists, synthesize their input, and ensure they had a voice in the future. The result was a new IS operating plan focused on getting the basics done right. We clearly communicated the work to be done, the organizational structure which supported that work and the right people to staff the structure. The next step was to implement the changes.

I've long been a fan of John Kotter and his work on leading change in organizations. His broad recommendations to effect change include:

a. Defrost the status quo
b. Take actions that bring about change
c. Anchor the changes in the corporate culture

The planning meetings described above defrosted the status quo. The actions I took to bring about change included:

Create a Vision for Change - the community came together with a vision of a web-centric organization and I broadly communicated it.

Establish a Sense of Urgency - everyone recognized that IT innovation was essential to coordinate clinical care, improve safety and enhance our competitiveness, especially after the merger of Beth Israel and Deaconess

Elicit Executive and Peer Sponsorship - The CEO declared that medication safety, personal health records, and enhanced communication to all levels of the organization were the strategic goals of the entire organization for that year

Communicate Vision to Implement Change - we established steering committees, project charters, project plans, and communication plans

Empower Employees to Implement Change - we aligned responsibility, accountability and authority throughout the IT organization so that managers had the resources and authority they needed to support our improvement efforts. We created a Special Projects team to coordinate the improvement projects without disrupting day to day operations.

Establish Short-term Goals - we created the first web application in healthcare to share data (with patient consent) among multiple organizations. We created the first web-based provider order entry system, and we created the first personal health record to share all hospital data with patients

Encourage Additional Changes - we created a non-punitive culture in which everyone was encouraged to identify mistakes and opportunities for process improvement

Reinforce Changes Made as Permanent - we built standard processes to deliver service, prioritize new projects, and communicate our multi-year plans to the community

That first year, we implemented strong project management methodologies, eliminated unnecessary work, and focused on getting basic services like email, networks, storage, and electronic result reporting rolled out to everyone in the community. Managing this work required resources, vision, and communication. All the pieces were in place to effect change.

Occasionally, I try to execute a change management project more quickly than usual, bypassing these steps. Whenever I do that I find that adoption of the new technology is delayed, budgets are at risk of overrun, and frustration escalates.

My decade of experience executing change suggests that Kotter was right. Building a guiding coalition, broadly communicating the vision, and celebrating a series of short term successes really works. I've watched projects without vision, resources or communication cause pain and anxiety throughout the organization. The good news is that we now know how to execute change and it is the role of senior management to enforce Kotter's principles in every change project.

LIFE AS AN HEALTHCARE CIO: The Role I Play (January 15 2014 post)

As 2014 begins, I marvel at the evolution of the CIO role from 1997 to 2014. Gone are the days when my role was to serve as technical expert, configuring web servers, optimizing data bases, or simplifying code. Gone are the days when product decision making depended on software architecture expertise to ensure scalability, reliability and security. Gone are the early wins of the "bold moves" like replacing Lotus Notes with Exchange, Novell with NT, Sybase with Microsoft SQL, and client/server with web applications.

Here are a few examples of the roles I play today from the past few weeks

1. Rethinking a challenging project by ensuring all stakeholders understand the key roles/responsibilities assigned during project formation i.e.

Defining the business champion
Defining the executive sponsor
Defining the role of IT
Defining the role of the project manager
Defining the support model
Defining the responsibility for creating, managing, and maintaining interfaces
Assigning responsibility for workflow/process definition
Assigning responsibility for vendor relationship management
Writing the governance committee charter
Defining the communication plan for internal and external customers
Defining unit testing and integrated testing responsibilities
Defining the training/education plan

2. Convening local government and provider stakeholders to

agree on a single approach for public health reporting that aligns meaningful use stage 2 requirements, healthcare information exchange timelines, and affordable care act planning. We needed consensus on scope, timing, and technical details so that local government efforts are complementary rather than competitive to the regulatory "must dos" of 2014

3. Presenting the BIDMC Enterprise IT strategy to senior leaders of the hospital and professional groups, so that all stakeholders understand the options, the decisions make thus far, and linkage between business requirements/IT tactics.

4. Serving as master of ceremonies for the statewide health information exchange public demonstration, ensuring all involved institutions were showcased to highlight their strengths.

5. Assisting with the development of new policies and procedures such as those involving privacy, healthcare information exchange and use of social media in healthcare

In 2014, the my work role has evolved to convener, communicator, mediator, navigator, and load balancer instead of technician, architect, programmer, informatician, and clinical expert. Not that the evolution is bad. In the modern era, we all have about 5 careers in our lives. What's amazing to me is how many careers I can have without changing my position as CIO!

I recently wrote a column for Information Week, Boiling the Frog describing some of the challenges all CIOs face as their roles evolve. As we begin 2014, I have the recovery time afforded by the holidays behind me and I'm approaching my role with new optimism. The chaos and stress of 2013 is behind me. I'm ready to thrive as I focus on using my evolving skills to make those who report to me as successful as possible.

Appendix to Chapter 25: Are medical devices really safe?

LIFE AS A HEALTHCARE CIO: The Security Risks of Medical Devices (February 27 2013 post)

Beth Israel Deaconess has been outspoken about the risks of malware on FDA 510k approved medical devices such as radiology workstations, echocardiogram machines, and patient monitors.

Although these devices appear to be "appliances" that you simply plug into the network and use for patient care, they are actually sophisticated computers, often running outdated versions of operating systems and applications that are not resilient against purposeful attacks.

For example, we have devices from a major manufacturer that internally use Windows NT as the operating system and Apache 1.0 as the web server. Patches are no longer available for these old versions of software and they cannot be updated to protect them from malware. Instead, we build hardware firewalls around the devices, creating "zero day" protection which mitigates risk by preventing internet-based attacks from reaching the devices.

In the past, manufacturers have claimed they cannot upgrade or patch software to enhance security because changing the device would trigger a new FDA 501k approval process.

Hence they have left the protection of the devices to the CIOs who manage hospital technology infrastructure.

In the past, when I've asked major device manufacturers to provide me a functional diagram of the ports and protocols used by their products that would enable me create tightly controlled firewalls, I've been told that the manufacturers do not have this information.

I've spoken to the FDA about this issue and they have advised me that device manufacturers have a responsibility to secure their products and there is no 510k re-certification needed when security patches are added. The FDA has wisely stated that there is shared responsibility. Device manufacturers must coordinate the updates and changes with hospital IT leaders and business owners. We have had circumstances where manufacturers serviced devices without IT knowledge and left them in a vulnerable state.

In November 2009, the FDA issued Reminder from FDA: Cybersecurity for Networked Medical Devices is a Shared Responsibility that reminded device manufacturers, hospitals, medical device users facilities, healthcare IT and procurement staff, medical device users, and biomedical engineers of the 2005 guidance as well as simple ways to protect against cybersecurity threats.

I've also talked to the FDA about including security penetration testing in the 510k process so that devices cannot be brought to market unless they are secure at baseline.

They have assured me that such regulations are in the planning phase. It is true that existing FDA regulations for device safety and efficacy never presumed that purposeful malware attacks would be an issue.

Here are other valuable references from the FDA

FDA issued guidance in 2005, Guidance to Industry – Cybersecurity for Networked Medical Devices Containing Off-the-Shelf (OTS) Software which answers question about pre-market review as well as other manufacturer responsibilities, such as validating software changes before releasing them.

At the same time as the guidance, the FDA issued Information for healthcare organizations about FDA's "Guidance for Industry: Cybersecurity for Networked Medical Devices Containing Off-the-Shelf (OTS) Software" that describes FDA's concerns about cybersecurity and what the guidance document covers.

In April 2005, the FDA hosted a webinar on the cybersecurity.

If your device manufacture claims the device cannot be patched due to FDA restrictions, refer them to these references and demand that devices be secured in collaboration with hospital IT staff and business owners. It a world of escalating malware, manufacturers have a duty to keep devices secure and safe.

Appendix to Chapter 28: Hospitals should be always ready for a disaster...

LIFE AS A HEALTHCARE CIO: Hospital Disaster Planning (July 18 2012 post)

In my role as CIO and a Professor of Medicine, I'm asked many questions about the policies, processes, and procedures of healthcare. Here's one I was recently asked about Hospital Disaster planning. Meg Femino, BIDMC Director of Emergency Management, prepared the answer.

The question:

Your hospital has been placed on alert for receiving patients from a local explosion at a large factory. Reports from the scene are spotty in terms of numbers killed or injured, and you do not know how many patients you may be getting. News reports are calling for casualties in the 100s, but local fire responders are sending in conflicting reports. You need to know what your ED will be receiving, so you can determine whether to close surgery to elective cases and to go on ED bypass for regular patients. Rumors are swirling inside the hospital and the chain of command about how severe the incident is and what it will do to your ability to function. What thoughts do you have about how to learn what you need to know in order to structure the hospital's preparations and continue regular functioning at the same time? What resources can you tap in order to learn more accurately about the situation at the scene and what you can expect to come to your ED? How would you manage this situation to cause the minimum disruption to regular hospital functioning?

When faced initially with a disaster situation in a health care setting, what do you think your first five steps need to be? Why?

Meg's answer:

This can be a common scenario, early information is always scant, unconfirmed and conflicting. Due to the mechanism of injury (explosion), chances are traumatic injuries will be present. That is what we would base our initial response on until credible information came in. We would immediately implement the following strategies:
* Activate the Emergency Operations Plan and the Incident Command System
* We would report to EMS via our disaster radio how many red (emergent), yellow (urgent) and green (non urgent) patients we can take. This is only a guide for EMS to distribute patients equally if they can, in a large mass casualty, you get what you get.
* Clear as many patients out of the Emergency Department as we could- admitted patients upstairs immediately, discharge others and decision make on the rest
* Alert the trauma teams with numbers expected, injuries, time to ED and any other pertinent information available
* Alert the OR's to hold any currently open rooms, do not start any other cases until we have more information and begin to assemble trauma teams. We know from previous drills we can open 17 OR rooms with staffed teams in 2 hours if we have to, this would involve canceling all non-emergent surgeries.
* We would see how many staffed in-patient beds are available in house and prepare for early discharges if we needed to. I call this the purge to surge.
* Alert the blood bank of potential incoming trauma to prepare for high volume of blood use
* Open the command center and assemble incident command team and begin gleaning information.

How we get information and share information during a citywide event:
* The Boston Hospitals have an emergency manager on call 24/7 for events like this. We would immediately be in touch with him, he liaisons with other citywide agencies and shares this information with hospitals.

* The TV provides information and usually pictures of the scene so we can get a better idea of the scope
* The city utilizes WebEOC which is a software system all hospitals, public safety, public health, EMS and others are linked in to. This system would be active within 15 minutes. Information is shared here across disciplines and is great for situational awareness. We can also share our situation with others, make resource requests and monitor others.
* Boston also has a medical intelligence center housed at Boston EMS, they would be pushing out information as it comes available. They would be asking our needs and monitoring the situation.
* We (hospital emergency managers) receive information messages from state agencies via the HHAN (Health and Homeland Alert Network), if they activate the state EOC etc.
* We also monitor the disaster radio in the ED, they will update us on how many more patients on scene, where they are going etc.

We flex our incident command team up or down as needed for response and tailor our response strategies to the needs of the event. As far as the five first steps I would say
1. Activation of the Emergency Operations Plan and notification Incident Command- this brings the team approach to the response
2. Preparing the hospital for patient surge
3. Gleaning information and sharing information to establish accurate situational awareness
4. Monitoring of resources- finding the balance with staffing and burn rates of supply. This allows you to continue treating and know when to call for more.
5. Stabilizing the event- treating those from the event to return the hospital to normal operations

AFTERWORD by Giuliano Pozza

As mentioned in the introduction, facts and characters in the novel are completely invented. I must say this is not in any way reassuring, since the appendices (both Life as a Healthcare CIO and FAQs & FACTS) demonstrate clearly that what is narrated in the novel is likely to happen or may have happened already. IT (or ICT, Information and Communication Technologies) is becoming more and more central in our personal and professional lives. IT is everywhere since it is behind every system managing information, plant automation, environment and building monitoring ... And the concern is valid for different contest. I started writing "The Fifth Domain" out of my experience but when I started collaborating with John I was astonished to discover so many common "pain points" even if our background and experiences are so different: I have been a CIO for a few years, he has been a CIO for almost 20 years. I am working in Italy, he is working in the USA. I am an ordinary CIO of a medium enterprise, he is one of the world leading CIOs of one of the most important healthcare institutions. I am managing a small budget and a small team, he is managing a vast and complex IT department ... but still when we started working together we found so many "common pain points". And we share even more common questions about the future.

In fact, we must acknowledge that unfortunately (or unwisely, I should probably say) the exorbitant technology development was not balanced with a growth in our capacity to govern it. As Dr. Bennato said, "A supplement of technology always needs a supplement of soul." It's only our capacity to govern our powerful instruments that prevent us from being manipulated by them. Shirley Turkle (I suggest everybody to read her book, "Alone Together") concluded that, observing externally, one could think the meaning of life of humans is to feed the gigantic social networks they built. Turkle is a psychologist who worked alongside technologists at MIT and U.S. technology users for most of her professional life: she gives us a pitiless picture of how incipient use of technology is changing (and generally not for the better) our personal lives and relationships.

At the enterprise level it is not much better. Well, we have a discipline about how to manage technology properly: IT Governance. But the level of consciousness about IT Governance principles among executives is disconcertingly low, as the capacity of IT professionals to communicate about IT governance principles is often low. There is a gap, very wide and very noticeable, between IT professionals and business executives when it comes to communication and listening styles. The gap is quite dramatic when it comes to IT governance, an area in which IT and non-IT executives need to communicate at least with a basic understanding of each other's positions. Besides, Aaron's story shows us how personal and enterprise levels can "meet" at times, with disastrous effects. One of my secret hopes, I must admit, is that this book could be useful in "reducing the gap" between different worlds and cultures. Sociologists would call it a "boundary object", a medium usable on both sides, enabling different cultures to start a fecund dialog.

One last note: I believe, leaving aside for a while our reflections on IT and IT Governance, that the 5 main characters of the book, Tommaso, Myriam, Martin, Ned and Diana, show us five talents we should never forget to use at their best: curiosity, humble and empathetic listening, communication skills, prudence and wisdom in the use of technology and strength of mind. I dare a last comment, saying that we need those gifts in all our endeavors in the present time. I am thinking specifically of my kids (some of them are actually young adults by now) and all of the young people I know. They will be asked to cope with a fast and interconnected (therefore unstable) world: they will need curiosity, humble and empathetic listening, communication skills, prudence and wisdom in the use of technology and strength of mind. All of the talents mentioned plus the passion and the sense of responsibility of the five characters will be vital for them to survive the challenges in front of them. Here now I am probably discovering my indirect fire. The endeavor is so vast we will perhaps need something more. We will need what Don Carlo, Myriam and Tommaso's friend, would call the "restoration of the human being." But this is probably a "Sixth Domain" of struggle, beyond the scope of this book.

ABOUT THE AUTHORS

Giuliano Pozza is the Chief Information Officer (CIO) of Fondazione Don Carlo Gnocchi Onlus, one of the largest social care and rehabilitation entities in Italy. Previously, Giuliano worked as the CIO of Istituto Clinico Humanitas and in the Health Care practice of consulting firm Accenture.

John D. Halamka, MD, MS, is a Professor of Medicine at Harvard Medical School, Chief Information Officer of Beth Israel Deaconess Medical Center, Chairman of the New England Healthcare Exchange Network (NEHEN), co-Chair of the US national HIT Standards Committee, and a practicing Emergency Physician.

Made in the USA
Charleston, SC
21 January 2014